HOOPS!

HOOPS!

CONFESSIONS OF A COLLEGE BASKETBALL ANALYST

BY

BILLY PACKER

WITH

ROLAND LAZENBY

CONTEMPORARY
BOOKS, INC.
CHICAGO

Library of Congress Cataloging in Publication Data

Packer, Billy.
   Hoops! : confessions of a college basketball analyst

     1. Packer, Billy.   2. Sportscasters—United States—
Biography.   3. Basketball—United States—History.
4. College sports—United States—History.   I. Lazenby,
Roland.   II. Title.
GV742.42.P33A34   1985   070.4'49796'0924   [B]   85-22443
ISBN 0-8092-5305-4

Published by Contemporary Books, Inc.
180 North Michigan Avenue, Chicago, Illinois 60601
Manufactured in the United States of America
Library of Congress Catalog Card Number: 8-22443
International Standard Book Number: 0-8092-5305-4

Published simultaneously in Canada by Beaverbooks, Ltd.
195 Allstate Parkway, Valleywood Business Park
Markham, Ontario L3R 4T8 Canada

To Barbara and the first people who should get into heaven—coaches' wives.

CONTENTS

FOREWORD

Call Billy Packer what you like. I prefer names like Loose Lips, Mothball Head, Ocean Mouth. Call him anything. But don't underestimate his basketball knowledge. Without a doubt, he's one of the most knowledgeable people in the game today. He gets offended if the game isn't coached right or played right. You can sense the irritation in his voice.

Nobody has his beliefs, his insight, his training, his positive attitude. He's probably been broadcasting basketball for 14 or 15 years, and throughout that time the man hasn't had fear. Most of your color people, your glamour-type broadcasters, have a fear of a sponsor or a coach or a network. They're afraid to say the things that might offend. Billy has no fear, no fear at all. He will say what he thinks. If you tell him it's wrong, he's still gonna say it. He believes it, so he says it. And I think that's the thing that makes Billy Packer so controversial. But if you're looking at it without tinted glasses, you'll find he shoots a tremendous percentage. I watched the Final Four this past year, and I was amazed at the accuracy of the things he said. His knowledge of the rule book is equal to just about any of the referees. Billy takes pride in that.

If Billy is open to any criticism, it's that he's too proficient, too technical, which sometimes leads him into dry areas, almost as if he's holding a basketball clinic. But to tell the truth, Billy knows the game, where I only feel it. Billy has tremendous input into a game for the people who know basketball. They're pleased by his knowledge.

But then Billy also shows the general viewers so many things they wouldn't otherwise see about the game. A lot of my stuff glitters. Billy's stuff is solid. Basketball is a fast-paced, sometimes complicated game. Billy sees everything, the coordination and passes. In our days together, I often didn't see things until the replays, and when the replays were shown, damnit, what he said was right. It's something he picked up from being around basketball so much. He's so enthusiastic about the game. Whenever I want to get rid of him I just stop talking basketball and he fades out, he just pouts a little bit and fades out.

Billy really helped me when I came along in broadcasting. At first, I didn't have his openness. When I first started I was the middle man on the NBC college basketball team. Billy and Dick Enberg would do the broadcasting, and I was called on for special comment. My face would appear in a little circle on the screen. It didn't work at all, and Billy said so. After about two games, he worked it so I sat in the broadcast booth with Dick and him. My coming into the booth opened up our act. We started to get established and pretty soon broke through the sound barrier.

A lot of people at NBC were uneasy about it. But we established a new tradition of broadcasting: open arguing, no holds barred. We actually went at each other and the audiences enjoyed it. I don't think that level can ever be reached again. We did it legitimately. We didn't plan or preconceive what we did. If some big story created differences of opinion, we didn't decide that one of us would take the pro and the other the con. For example, with Larry Bird, we never said, "Hey, you talk about how good he is and I'll talk about how he's overrated." Billy thought Bird was a bit overrated and I thought he was great. Our debates were always natural offshoots of our beliefs. But then after we sensed the debate, we milked it.

Dick Enberg was the pro who kept us within the rules. Usually in basketball broadcasting, there's no room for three people. But we made the perfect threesome. When our team broke up after 1981 and Billy went to CBS, I think the losers were mainly the viewers.

We both have moved along in our careers. Even though we work for different networks, we're still like an odd couple. We're extremely close. I just enjoy being with Billy Packer, the fact that he doesn't get wrapped up in the limo and suite syndrome. He's never turned Hollywood. If anything, he's the opposite of that. It's remarkable that somebody with the television exposure he gets has never moved onto the stage. You'll never see a gold chain around Billy's neck. He's straight laced. I can verify it even though he hurts my style. He's moral almost to the point that it's hard for anyone younger than 35 to understand his style of life. He's not for the yuppies.

I think that he's an aware and concerned person who at times gets very stubborn. But being stubborn is one of his big assets. Most talented people are very stubborn. And confident. . . . He has a tremendous amount of self-confidence. Under no condition will he put on makeup. If anybody needs help before the cameras, it's him, but he just won't put on the makeup. He thinks it's feminine. He's so macho. He's the manly style. I don't think Billy ever had his hair cut or dressed a certain way for the TV audience. What you see is what you get. He's an extremely loyal person. If you had to spend some time in a foxhole or in no-man's-land, you'd want him around.

I guess you can view him this way: Billy's no buffalo chips. He'll take something to drink now and then, but it's very rare, usually something sweet, like some hooker would drink, something way out. No one will dance with him he's so homely. But he's just a complete joy. Dick and I both miss him.

The more I think about it, Billy's the Middle American

type. Basketball and business. Still, he isn't going to pick up his meal check unless you go to the washroom with him and wait for him to come out.

We had great fun in our days working together. I think we communicated some of that fun to our viewers. This book reflects the good time we had following college basketball. Whatever Billy says about me is true. But more than the funny stuff and gags, this book gives a sense of Billy's great love for the game. Read it, and you'll come away with a greater appreciation of it yourself. Billy's not always right. Nobody is. But he always has good insight.

Al McGuire

ACKNOWLEDGMENTS

The authors would like to thank their wives, Barbara Packer and Karen Lazenby, for their work in preparing the manuscript. They would also like to thank Tom Merrit of NBC and Smith Barrier for help in obtaining information used in the book.

HOOPS!

CHAPTER

1

MY PAL AL

The first time I met Al McGuire was toward the close of the 1974–75 season. I was assigned to cover an NBC regional game in Tuscaloosa, Alabama, where Kentucky was playing Marquette, McGuire's team. Kentucky, of course, eventually moved on to the NCAA finals. McGuire was important to basketball in 1975, but he was still a regional item then, something of an oddity.

The day before the game, we watched the two teams practice. The Marquette practice was an experience. This guy McGuire was a real wacko. All he did was shout at the guys and walk around with this little stick in his hand. He really didn't have a handle on things, in my opinion. His assistant, Hank Raymonds, seemed to be running the show. All Al did was scream at the guys every once in a while. He chased Earl Tatum out of practice that day, and Earl was his star player. I thought "Boy, this guy McGuire is really a weirdo."

At the game the next day, the broadcast booth was set up so that I was sitting right next to McGuire and the Marquette bench. Al had a lot of skinny kids on his team. Lloyd Walton,

1

the point guard, weighed about 140 pounds. And Kentucky had a bruising team with Rick Robey and Mike Phillips coming off the bench. It was a powerful team, and Joe B. Hall had installed a power game. Al's team opened a lead, 23–17 or so, and then Hall put in his bruisers, Rick Robey and Mike Phillips. Suddenly, the game got real violent. The Kentucky boys started knocking people around, and the refs weren't calling any fouls. McGuire screamed at the refs and raised hell. I thought "This character McGuire is absolutely crazy. Why doesn't he sit down and coach the game? He's got his team in good shape."

Then, all of a sudden, when his team was still in the lead, he sat down and said to Raymonds, "This game's over. The hell with it, Hank. You take it the rest of the way."

He had the lead, and he didn't do another thing for the rest of the game. I was stunned. "That dumb son of a gun," I said to myself. "If he'd stayed in there and coached, his team would have won the game."

I really had a negative opinion of him. He was a wacko, a pain in the ass. That guy wasn't taking a team anywhere. I thought he had abused his team in practice and treated his assistant coaches terribly. He was a pain with the referees, but worse, he'd quit in the game. Since that time I have come to understand that that is simply Al McGuire. Al, in his own mind, has life so simplified. He is so smart that he realized, if the referees were going to let that game get rough, no matter how hard they played, his kids eventually would lose. They wouldn't be able to play a wide-open game against Kentucky. He needed the game to be closely called. He needed a lot of touch fouls that would allow his players to work their finesse. And the minute the referees let the play get physical, Al decided, "Why should I get all excited about this game? I'm not going to win it." Basically, he relaxed the rest of the game. Now that I know him so well, I can appreciate where he was coming from. But back then I thought the guy was an idiot.

NBC covered his team again during the 1977 regular season. Marquette was floundering terribly early that year.

In fact, the team appeared to be headed toward Al's poorest season on record. We did a game between the University of Cincinnati and Marquette in Cincinnati. It was one of the worst games we did all year. Cincinnati won. Marquette played horribly. It was just a bad game, the kind a broadcaster really hates to do. When it was over, I felt sorry for McGuire. He had recently announced his retirement. He'd been an outstanding coach. I couldn't help thinking of the '75 NCAA game and the way he had acted. But he was a character and a bit of a renegade, and he'd been a hell of a coach at Belmont Abbey, a small school in North Carolina. I'd been in college when he was coaching there, but I didn't know the guy. And I still didn't when I became a broadcaster. I'd covered one of his games, but it wasn't like I'd go up and say, "Al, how ya doin'?"

Yet when this Cincinnati game was over, I felt like speaking to him, knowing that he was in his last season and things weren't going well. At that point, his team was near .500 on the season. So I decided I'd go in after the game and congratulate him on a fine career—you know, say I enjoyed doing his ball game and wish him the best of luck in the future. But he wasn't in the locker room. I found out that he'd already gone out to the bus, so I went outside to find him. He was there in the front seat of the bus eating a peanut butter sandwich out of a plastic wrapper. I figured he'd be all pissed off over the loss, but he wasn't at all. I gave my little speech, and he just sat there impatiently saying, "Yeah, OK, great to see you, too. OK, fine." His tone was like, "Get the hell off the bus. We're getting ready to leave."

There I was, showing all this empathy for this guy. I was trying to cheer him up, and he kicks me off the bus. As the bus pulled away, I stood out in the street, thinking what an idiot I was. "The hell with that guy. I mean, what a jerk. His team's horseshit anyway. He's lucky we even put them on the air. I shouldn't have even wasted my time to see the guy. He wouldn't have done the same for me." That was the end of Al McGuire as far as I was concerned. I didn't want to see him again. Ever.

Then, all of a sudden, his team went to Virginia Tech and won a game. I was keeping up with his scores—not because I thought they were going anywhere, just out of curiosity. The win surprised me. Then they kept winning, and the next thing I knew, they had a pretty good win streak going. They made it to the Midwest Regional championship against my alma mater, Wake Forest. And Marquette won the game. Suddenly, they were in the Final Four. I hadn't even had a chance to cover them in the NCAA tournament.

Of course, that was one of the most dramatic Final Fours I've seen, especially the last game. Here's this guy McGuire who's captivated the fans. And nobody knows where his team is staying. All the news media hammered John Thompson for not telling where his team was housed during the 1982 Final Four. Back in 1977, not only did the press not know where Al's team was, they didn't know where in the hell *he* was. He was out with a friend riding motorcycles.

Here's this Al McGuire in the Final Four. He ain't gonna win it, but he's in it. Then he goes on and captures that game against UNC Charlotte with Jerome Whitehead scoring as the buzzer sounds. There's a brief controversy as to whether the bucket should count. The referee rules it good, and Marquette is in the championship. It's exciting as hell. It made great drama for our NBC broadcasting team, which then consisted of Dick Enberg, Curt Gowdy, John Wooden, and me.

That Sunday, we had McGuire and North Carolina's Dean Smith, the championship coaches, come in for an interview on what to expect at the Monday night game. That was really the first time I ever spent any time around McGuire. Before, he had never been around, never accessible to anybody. He'd whisk into a game, and then he'd be gone. A wacko mystery figure. That Sunday, he appeared in an old black turtleneck. He was wearing sneakers and old beat-up pants. Just a damn ratty-looking guy, just terrible. And as usual, Dean Smith had everything perfect. With Dean, we had to do the interview a couple of times because it needed to be just right for the Carolina image. And then McGuire came in, and he was off the wall with all his bullshit and all his lingo and everything. Funny as hell. Again I said to myself, "This guy's got no handle on what the hell he's doing, but he is damn neat entertainment."

Obviously, he was what the networks wanted. He was unique. Whether he lasted didn't matter. He was a guy the networks could sell. Then he goes and wins the national championship. More than that, he wins with such dramatic fashion, and he breaks down at the end, and he cries, and it's his last game, and he's retiring, and he's turned his team around, and his family comes down on the court to celebrate. He does all these great things. They happen right in front of the cameras. Overnight, he's a media superstar.

I was supposed to go down and do a postgame interview, but we had no rapport because I could never get to him. At practice, he wasn't the kind of coach you could talk to or discuss basketball with or anything because he wasn't accessible. He was so far removed from the typical coach. I chased him across the floor that day, and he never even turned around. I couldn't even get him. He was running all over the place, his hair all messed up. I don't think we ever got him on camera for an interview.

Then, lo and behold, the next thing I hear, NBC's thinking about hiring Al McGuire. That was in 1977, right after his Marquette team won the championship. "What the hell will he do?" I asked myself. "What is he going to add?" I didn't understand the entertainment side of the business. He was perfect for NBC. And it eventually turned out that he was perfect to become part of our broadcast threesome—Enberg, McGuire, Packer.

At first, I was upset that the guy was going to be involved in what I did, because I didn't think he knew much about basketball broadcasting. I had never heard him talk about basketball. Usually, he just said weird stuff about aircraft carriers and things like that. I didn't feel threatened. I just didn't see how it could work out. As a matter of fact, neither did Al.

When the network people first called him in to discuss his

becoming an NBC broadcaster, Al had his doubts. "How can you hire me?" he asked. "I don't even know how to pronounce words right."

And they said, "Well, we'll help you."

"How the hell can you help me?" he asked. "This is the way I talk. I've been talking this way all my life. You can't help me. What'll I do?"

They said, "Well, you know, it'll work out. Don't worry about it."

Scotty Connal, then one of the top people in NBC sports, called me and told me not to worry about things because Dick Enberg and I would continue our broadcast teamwork. Connal said McGuire would be in a "coaches' box" in the locker room, where he'd watch the game on monitors. When Al saw something he wanted to comment on, or when something witty came to mind, Al was to press a button. A light would then come on in our broadcast booth, and Dick would lead him into the broadcast. Al's image would be superimposed on the screen. The setup would allow him to comment while the game was in progress. Also, Al was scheduled to do halftime shows, "On the Road with Al McGuire" or something like that.

That sounded OK to Dick and me. Our first game turned out to be the Cuban national team against Marquette in Milwaukee. Here we were in Milwaukee, which is Al's home. The Marquette people were going to honor him by unveiling the national championship banner at the game. It was 1978, and the game was the first time Cubans had played a sporting event in America since Castro's revolution. There was a lot of tension as to whether somebody might try to cause trouble. Dick and I had traveled in together. We didn't say anything, but we anticipated a little hospitality from Al. There was nothing. Al never invited us to come to his house. He never mentioned going out to dinner with us, showing us a good restaurant, introducing us to some of his friends. We never saw the guy. He was a total stranger, almost like the enemy.

But it was a big emotional thing for him to be back there.

And we didn't know it at the time, but Al had no intention of ever going to another basketball game. Not anywhere, much less in Milwaukee. And he didn't go to games unless he had to broadcast them. It's not his hobby to watch basketball games. To this day, he doesn't watch basketball. He never watched when he was a coach. His interests were in other things: collecting toy soldiers and other off-the-wall stuff.

All those factors made for a very strained opening in Milwaukee. Dick and I did our broadcast thing, and Al pushed his button every once in a while. But, in our opinion, he added nothing to the broadcast. He looked nice, and he said goofy things, but that's all. Dick and I talked about how poorly the setup worked. It wasn't smooth at all. We decided it would be better if Al came out of the locker room and sat with us in the booth. "Let's get him out here," we said. "Then we can at least keep up with him."

We took our idea to the producer, and Dick orchestrated the whole thing for the next game. He led the band, and Al and I chimed in whenever we thought we should say something. It worked out fine. At the time, we didn't even know why it worked. You would assume there would be some big ego problems with the three of us stepping all over each other's toes. Because neither of us knew Al very well, Dick and I tended to lean toward each other. Al was somewhat left out. He was basically a loner. We didn't spend much time together. And when Al did spend time with us, it was almost like he hated doing it.

Then, after the first few weeks, we started clicking a little bit. Things started happening. Al would say some things, and I would go back at him. Or he would come back at me. In those first weeks, we were adversaries. We didn't know each other. We weren't friends. All we had were our differences of opinion. And we had those. Al and I are as different as night and day in our opinions about basketball, our basic interest in the game. We'd have these spontaneous exchanges, and both of us kind of got our feathers up a little bit. I didn't give a damn what he had ever done. I didn't care if he had coached a national championship team. He didn't know what was going on out on the floor during our broadcasts. And Al, from the opposite standpoint, was saying, "What did this guy Packer ever do to have an opinion?" It was almost like, "Hey, kid, where do you get this stuff you're coming up with about the game?"

The friction was created by a genuine disagreement on the issues. First, our backgrounds were so different. Al was from the East and played his college ball at St. John's, an independent school in those days. I played in the South, at Wake Forest, in the Atlantic Coast Conference. My orientation was toward the success of a great conference.

During my college years in the early 1960s, Al had his first head coaching job at Belmont Abbey College, a small independent school near Charlotte, North Carolina. Belmont Abbey had an excellent team during Al's tenure. Yet regardless of the coaching job he did, Al would always be considered a minor item, because his team played in Carolina, the hotbed of the ACC. That had to weigh on his mind a little bit. Frank McGuire was getting all the hoopla and attention at the University of North Carolina, not Al McGuire at Belmont Abbey College. Al appeared to be a wacky guy at a nice little school who was pretty good, but no big news. Al was no different from the other coaches in the region. Anybody who is ever in ACC country and is really not part of the ACC action has a little bone to pick, a little resentment toward the publicity the league gets. Coaches like Al had the feeling that everything was overrated and overplayed. That only made his 1977 national championship win over North Carolina that much sweeter.

When Al left Belmont Abbey, he went to Marquette, another independent school, sitting right in the heartland of Big 10 basketball. Al has a tremendous combative and competitive nature. When those juices get to flowing, he fears nothing. That was reflected in his teams. At Marquette, he launched a one-man crusade for the independent schools. He was very defensive about the schedule Marquette played. He didn't think much of postseason conference tournaments and the trend toward the NCAA selecting several teams from one conference for the tournament. Al thought most conference powerhouses got 50 percent of their wins against patsies and weaker conference teams.

I believed just the opposite, that conference rivalries made those games more difficult. The independent schools could always schedule around other good teams, but the conference schools had to play them. We both had valid opinions based on our experience. That made for strong arguments and good chemistry. There were things I didn't understand about independents, and there were things about conferences Al didn't understand. Our debate was the same one that for years had been carried out in bars and living rooms, wherever people watched basketball. People just weren't used to hearing the same argument from game commentators. Instead of everything being nice and slick, we had a red-hot debate going. The electricity between Al and me could be felt by the audience. Dick Enberg was perfect at keeping that chemistry going or getting it started. At times he would try to get us going at each other. He would be like a referee at a key boxing match. If the fight was going well, he stayed out. "Don't screw it up," was his philosophy. He was the catalyst for everything.

I'll never forget a game we did between Ohio State and Virginia in 1980. Terry Holland, the Virginia coach, had a strategy of substituting defensive players for offensive players near the end of the game. If the other team had the ball, Holland put in his defensive players. And when Virginia got the ball back, Holland put the scorers back in the game. Holland had Jeff Lamp on his team in those days, and with a minute 40 or so left in the game, he pulled Lamp out and put in a defensive player. Al was shocked and criticized Holland. I told Al he didn't know what he was talking about. Holland was making a good tactical move.

"Aw, Billy, you're crazy," Al shot back. "Man, that's the dumbest thing I ever heard. That coach ought to be fired." Then Al moved his chair away from the broadcast table and sat back. "I'm not working this game," he said and left the broadcast booth. He went and sat with the fans. Dick and I finished the game. Virginia lost, and not a lot more was said.

Al usually didn't want to talk about basketball off camera. It just didn't interest him that much. But the next day we were walking outside our hotel, and he asked about the coaching move. I explained it again, and Al said, out of the blue, "You know, I shouldn't get on Barry that bad."

I said, "Who's Barry?"

He said, "You know."

And I said, "No, I don't know the guy." I thought he was off on some tangent about business or something. Al has a way of changing subjects quickly.

"You know," he said, "the coach from Virginia, the tall guy who used to work with Lefty Driesell at Davidson."

"Oh, you mean Terry. Terry Holland," I said.

"Yeah, Terry," he said. "That's his name, Terry." That was so typical of Al. He could care less what Holland's name was. But Al could get by with not knowing it because the fans out there in television land knew this was Al McGuire.

That kind of thing happened all through the first year. Slowly, we learned to laugh about it. We realized we didn't have a hang-up with each other. Our arguments were genuine. Al doesn't like too many people around him, but eventually he gained confidence as a broadcaster, and all three of us started to feel we were becoming a good broadcast team.

I began thinking, "Hey, this guy McGuire is really smart, but he's smart for different reasons." And I think Al thought, "Hey, maybe this guy Packer wasn't a super coach or a name player, but the little bastard knows something about the game." Those feelings brought us closer together. Dick was still orchestrating the threesome, but Al and I were becoming tight friends.

Still, the development of my relationship with Al McGuire took some funny turns. Actually, they might be considered downright odd. We had been on the West Coast doing a UCLA game and were scheduled to do a promo show for the upcoming NCAA tournament. Dick, Al, and I were to forecast which teams, players, and coaches would be the hot items. The show was scheduled to be shot at four different locations in southern California, with each setting representing one of the four basketball regions: East, Mideast, Midwest, and West. Our first stop was Will Roger's home. Our next site was the beach at Santa Monica.

Al informed us he didn't care what we did or when we started, but from noon until two o'clock he would be unavailable. Dick and I didn't give it too much thought. We figured Al had an appointment, and NBC scheduled a shooting break at noon anyway. So what the hell?

For each location, we were supposed to dress differently. Although the NBC people said things would be very casual, Al told me to make sure I brought a coat and tie. I figured Al knew something I didn't, so I brought the extra clothes. At Will Rogers's farm, we wore blue jeans for the country effect. Dick looked supergood, but Al was real concerned that I didn't look sharp enough. He tried to change my shirt, and I got a little annoyed with him. I thought I looked all right. "I'm not supposed to look as good as Dick anyway," I said, "and you're no great picture to look at in your outfit." Somehow we got through the session at Rogers's home.

From there we moved on to the beach at Santa Monica, where we were supposed to wear real casual clothes. Al, who was employed as an assistant to the president at Medalist Industries, brought out some Medalist jogging outfits and asked us to wear them. They fit both Dick and me, but Dick had brought along some nice-looking casual clothes that fit him better. So Dick wore his own clothes, which miffed Al because Dick looked a lot better in the clothes than I did. Al said the Medalist image would be ruined because they had me, a Polack, wearing them. We proceeded to shoot the segment, and as we got closer and closer to noon, Al became more anxious and less interested in making sure we were picking the right teams in the right regions.

He was really hustling everybody along. When we goofed, he said, "We don't need to take that over again. That take was good." Dick started it again with me. "OK, Billy," he said, "What teams are strong in the East Regional?" I mentioned a couple of teams. Then Dick asked Al what he thought.

"I don't care," Al said hastily. "I think Furman will win it all."

I looked over and said, "Al, you've got to be crazy. Why are you talking about Furman?"

He said, "That's my pick, and I've got to go." With that, the session ended. As he left, Al said, "Come on. You've got to go with me." I didn't have any idea where we were going. We ran up to the car, and Al said, "I'm really going to be late. I'm in trouble here."

Unfortunately, I had locked the keys in the trunk of the rented car. Also in the trunk were our dress clothes. I didn't know what we were going to use them for. Al hadn't bothered to explain that he had scheduled a meeting at the Beverly Wilshire Hotel with a large number of key Los Angeles area stockbrokers. As the featured speaker at the meeting, he planned to make a sales pitch on behalf of Medalist Industries. He hadn't asked the network people for time off because he thought they wouldn't approve it. And he had already plugged the event into his schedule.

But here we were with the keys locked in the trunk. Al waved down a cop, borrowed his crowbar to tear the trunk top off our rented car, and we drove down Santa Monica Boulevard at about 100 miles an hour, with Al changing clothes in the back seat. He was determined he wasn't going to miss the meeting.

Well, we made it just in time. Those stockbrokers and high rollers would never have guessed Al had just come from a mad dash down the freeway. He opened his talk by saying to the audience, "I'm no brassiere up here talking to you. I'm not just something up front. I'm really involved with this company."

The crowd loved it. Al was a smashing success, and I tried not to look too ridiculous in a Medalist jogging outfit.

Al McGuire is completely unique. Unfortunately, he and Medalist eventually severed their ties. In my opinion, the company was the loser in that one. The people who deal with Al McGuire have to take the time to understand him. If Medalist Industries had only started a division called Al

McGuire Enterprises, the company could have used his talents to the fullest and probably reaped some nice profits. Instead, they expected him to blend into corporate America.

Of course, if Al *had* been a true corporate animal, he probably wouldn't have exercised the creative instincts he applied so successfully in working with Medalist. I remember one incident that was a perfect example of Al's ingenuity in publicity.

A lot of people remember that Marquette University had very unusual uniforms, though nobody really understood why they always changed their uniforms at certain key times. For example, when they went to Madison Square Garden, they showed up with their bumblebee uniforms— those striped ones. When they got on national television, they would break out another new uniform, and everybody talked about how they had shirts that hung over the pants.

Well, I never knew why Al changed his team's uniforms so often, but I thought maybe he did it to psych up the players. As it turned out, it had nothing to do with that.

Medalist Industries, whom Al worked for even when he was a coach, makes uniforms. One of the things Al could do for the company was say, "Hey, next year I'm going to be on the TV X number of times. You guys give me some new uniforms, and I'm going to get a hell of a lot of advertising for you." Al's never told me this, but I know him well enough now to know where he was coming from. And he arranged an incredible display. He would be all over TV, and the broadcasters would be talking about the new uniforms and showing them on camera. There was never any mention of Medalist, but, of course, Medalist could play right off that. What do you think networks would have charged Medalist Industries to display their new uniforms to the national audience?

So, we did the first game Al ever broadcast with us, in 1978. Al had worked a deal with Marquette, and the school broke out new uniforms at the opening game against Notre Dame.

Now, Notre Dame's Digger Phelps is one of the shrewdest guys in the business, and he realizes Marquette is going to change uniforms, so *he* decides to display some new uniforms for the game too.

When we got to the game Dick Enberg heard about Notre Dame's new uniforms and Marquette's new uniforms, so he says, "Let me do the pregame show as a fashion show." Al, of course, loved it. Not only is he going to get new uniforms shown at the game, but the whole pregame show is going to be a showcase for the uniforms.

Well, Dick goes out and gets Butch Lee from Marquette and Duck Williams from Notre Dame out on the floor and orchestrates a fashion show. Without even knowing it, Dick gave Al McGuire and Medalist Industries another opportunity to get three, four, or five minutes free air time.

The assets that make Al so valuable are intangible. He always knows what he wants, and he has an uncanny sense of where to look for it and how to get it. It's fortunate for both Al and the people around him that he doesn't have any great material interest. Otherwise, he'd be an absolute killer as a businessman. Or somebody would have killed him by now.

When Al *does* know what he wants, watch out. Nothing will stop him.

Al gets a real kick out of shopping for toy soldiers and antiques. We spent an awful lot of time on the road at flea markets and antique shops, which I must admit I enjoyed too. Nobody strikes a harder bargain at a flea market than Al McGuire. Those goofy toy soldiers he collects can range anywhere from $2.75 to $15.00. Al likes to buy them for $1.80. We looked long and hard for them, and even now that we don't travel together, I keep my eyes open for bargains for him.

Well, back in 1978, NBC had the misfortune—and the network should have know better—of booking a basketball game in an arena where a flea market was also being held. In Kentucky, the Louisville fairgrounds arena has often hosted ball games and flea markets simultaneously. The combination was disastrous for Al because he spent most of his time over at the flea market and very little time thinking about basketball.

The NBC people weren't expecting the same problems when we did a game at Rupp Arena in 1979. But a flea market was set up in the shopping area next to the arena. And sure enough, we walked in the wrong door on our way to practice the day before the game and found ourselves right in the midst of the flea market. Al said, "Oh, we've got to spend some time there."

"Al," I said, "We've got to hurry to get to practice, but do what you want to do." He took one end of the arena, and I took the other end, and we planned to meet in the middle. We proceeded to case the place for any bargains. Well, when we got to the middle, I'd found a few things that were worth coming back for the next day. Al was ecstatic over a toy truck that he had found.

"You've got to come and see this truck," he said. "It's just a great little truck." He sometimes buys antique toys and then trades them with people for toy soldiers. We went back to this stall, and there was a real nice truck there. But the owner wanted about $75 for it. That was way over the amount of money Al would ever want to spend on any antique toys or soldiers. He'll trade for them, but he doesn't like to spend that kind of cash. The guy who operated the booth and his wife didn't know Al McGuire or Billy Packer from Adam. They were really into antiques, but not into basketball, which is hard to find in the state of Kentucky. So Al wasn't really able to charm them. They knew what the truck was worth, and they were going to get their money for it. Al said, "Well, you just think about it. If you don't sell it, I'll be back tomorrow." The next day was game day, and I wondered when Al was going to get time to get back into a hassle with this fellow over the price of that toy truck.

The next day, we did the game, and when it was over, we had quite a bit of time to fill. The producers sent me down to one end of the court to interview some players, and Al was sent to the other end for more interviews. I went down, took my broadcast position, and interviewed the players. As I talked to them, I could hear the director saying through my earpiece, "Now let's throw it down to Al McGuire." I looked down to the other end, and Al was nowhere to be found. So I kept right on going with the interview until it was time for a commercial break. I signed into the break, and people started asking me, "Where's McGuire? What's happened to him?"

"I don't know," I said. "He's not here."

We had another couple of minutes to fill, and the producers said, "You just carry it from here and take it by yourself."

I agreed and threw it back to Dick once and then did a few more interviews. Finally, the show ended and we went off the air. I started thinking that Al hadn't said anything to me, and he knew where we were supposed to go. I thought maybe he had gotten sick. It's very strange for him just to take off like that. We went back to the truck, and Al wasn't there. I was really starting to worry about him. Then, all of a sudden, it struck me: Could he possibly have taken off and gone to that flea market before we were off the air? I hustled through the gym doors in Rupp Arena that led to the exhibition space next door. Just as I got to the exhibition space, there, sitting on the steps in front of the doors, was Al McGuire playing with that little truck.

He looked up when he saw me coming. "I got it," he said, "for 45 bucks."

From top to bottom, Al's first year with us was crazy, with the Final Four in St. Louis capping off everything. On Saturday morning, the network brass called us in early for some unknown reason. Dick, Al, and I were left for three hours sitting on these stools. We hadn't been there long when this guy walks by and says, "I want you guys up for today's game. I want you really interested. C'mon now, let's really be fired up. Let's have a good day out of you guys." This fellow, whoever he was, had on blue jeans and a sweater. He was an unshaven but nice-looking sort of guy. But we didn't pay much attention to him. About half an hour later the same guy came by and got us from behind grabbing us by the necks. "Hey, guys, really get fired up," he said.

And we thought, "What are you talking about?" We were hours from game time. What was the need to get excited? Al looked over to the camera guys and said, "Will somebody get this guy a blow job?"

Things got real uneasy. Nobody laughed, and the reason was that the guy was Don Ohlmeyer, the executive producer at NBC who had just come to the network from ABC to head up the 1980 Olympics. Then Ohlmeyer started laughing, because he thought Al was just kidding. But Al wasn't kidding. Al wanted whoever the hell this guy was to get out of there. He was irritated at having to sit there for three hours.

The next morning, Sunday, was in the Easter season, and I decided to attend Mass at a little chapel under the big arch in St. Louis. It was kind of cold, but the chapel wasn't too far from our hotel, so I walked down there. I sat in the back of this little church, and during the service, I noticed that there were all kinds of people there. There were vagrants and street people and people dressed nicely. Just a real mixture. I noticed that one guy who sat several rows in front of me was dressed like a bum. He had an old stocking cap pulled down over his head. As I walked back down the aisle from Communion, I glanced at the guy's face and realized, "Damn, that was Al." I had on my coat and tie and was dressed as nice as could be.

We had been working much better together by then, but we still didn't have what you'd call a friendship. When Mass was over, I waited for him outside. We took a walk together, the first of many over the next few years. But this was the first one, when we really began to know one another. On this cold Sunday morning, we went down to the wharf on the Mississippi River, where a row of boats were tied up. A couple of the boats were floating restaurants. Al, with his beat-up clothes and ski cap, suddenly began hollering at these guys working on one of the boats. They came over to us, and Al told them he was from the city sanitation department and he was there to check them out. He's screaming at these guys, so they let us on the boat, where he tells them he wants to check out the kitchen. He goes back there, raising all kinds of hell. "Get this clean," he tells them. They think I'm an inspector, too. We tour the whole boat, and Al warns them, "I'll be back. I want this done by tomorrow."

The whole scene was absolutely absurd. We were like two college kids pulling some prank. I laughed my ass off, and the whole incident kind of sealed our friendship.

There was a funny postscript to that particular year. The season ended, and Al, being a shrewd businessman, realized that he had been paid only to do the halftime shows and sit in the coaches' box for occasional comments. That had all changed after the first game, so he decided to send NBC a bill for announcing the games too. Because he was paid to make a certain number of appearances for the network, he figured the halftime show counted as an appearance and announcing the game counted as another one. The bill called for NBC to double the payment. When it arrived, it all hit the fan at NBC. "Who authorized this?" the executives asked. Of course, nobody authorized paying Al McGuire double. So the network brass finally called in everybody to see who was going to take the brunt of the responsibility for bringing McGuire into the broadcast booth.

On one hand, the change had worked very well. Our threesome had gotten tremendous notoriety. Some critics had gone so far as to say we had helped increase the popularity of the college game. On the other hand, there was a $30,000 bill to pay. Knowing that the amount of money that eventually was going to be generated by the popularity of college basketball made $30,000 seem like change for coffee and doughnuts, Al was hoping that they would send him some extra money. He really didn't think they were going to send him all of it.

But the network people called in their lawyers. They think Al's out there with some lawyer ready to come down on their heads. All he's really doing is hoping he can rip them off for a few thousand dollars. But none of us knew him that well at the time. So the lawyers decided that yes, he did work, and NBC had to pay him.

Like I said, Al's a real killer.

CHAPTER

2

SCANDAL

Al McGuire always criticizes me for being the kind of guy who throws a beer party at his house and then locks all the bathroom doors. That would be the same kind of guy who would want to rehash the worst moments in the history of college basketball. If that's the case, then so be it, because those moments should never be forgotten. They involve what I call basketball's "Hall of Shame." And maybe it's important to me because basketball's worst moments touched my life and those of dozens of other college players.

What I'm talking about, of course, are the point shaving investigations of the early 1960s. If you were a college player in those days, as I was, the investigations had a way of getting your attention.

They smacked me right in the face in the spring of 1961, just days after I completed my junior season as a guard at Wake Forest. I grew up in a family surrounded by basketball. My father was a college coach at Lehigh. But in 1961 I knew nothing of the gambling scandals that had rocked collegiate basketball just 10 years earlier. I was like most other young college players: a little naïve, preoccupied with things more interesting. Our age group had been in grade school when the 1950s scandal broke. The Korean War was going on. America was getting ready to elect Ike. But things like gambling scandals, wars, and even presidential elections were far removed from our little worlds.

Names of the great basketball stars of the 1950s—Lane, Melchiorre, Groza, and Beard—could just as well have been partners in a law firm as famous athletes. Kids my age hadn't heard of them. Their stories weren't glorified; their names weren't passed on to the Hall of Fame. They were superstars who never got to play in the NBA. They were the outlaws of college basketball, not meant to be remembered. And like them, some of the collegiate superpowers of the 1950s, teams like City College of New York and Long Island University, were knocked from prominence by a stigma that threatened even Kentucky and Adolph Rupp. A decade later, CCNY and LIU weren't to be found in the sports pages on the Top 20 lists with other big-time schools. By 1961, they no longer had the type of basketball program that would send high school athletes recruiting brochures. For all intents and purposes, those schools had been wiped off the face of the basketball world.

In the early 1960s, gambling was pretty much a behind-the-scenes practice. That might seem hard to believe today, with newspapers, TV commentators, and magazine tip sheets regularly publicizing, even promoting, the point spreads for college games. But in my innocent college days, talk of gambling was as uncommon as a two-handed slam dunk. Thinking back, I don't believe I'd even heard of a point spread when I went to college. That may seem strange, with my having grown up in Bethlehem, Pennsylvania, just 80 miles from New York City.

For me, the age of innocence came to a grinding halt in March of 1961. That month, all of my concentration was focused on trying to help Wake Forest get into the Final Four. That's when the news first broke that two Seton Hall players, Hank Gunter and Art Hicks, had admitted their involvement in fixing games. News reports said an investigation was reaching throughout the college basketball hierarchy, shaking the lives of big-name coaches and players. It had begun six months earlier, when New York detectives began tailing Aaron "The Bagman" Wagman as he traveled around the country paying a total of $30,000 to basketball players to fix games. Before the investigation was through, it would draw me in as well.

The first news about Seton Hall really hit me hard because Al Senavitas, my best friend from childhood and high school, was an outstanding player for Seton Hall. I remember hoping Al wasn't involved. I had seen him just two weeks earlier when our teams were both playing at Madison Square Garden. He didn't seem aware of the investigation at the time. If he had been, I think he would have said something about it. The Seton Hall case was a textbook example of fixing. The fixer in that game, Joseph Hacken, had paid Gunter and Hicks to beat the point spread in a Seton Hall game against Dayton in Madison Square Garden. Dayton was favored to win by six, but Hacken had bet that the margin would be greater. With Gunter and Hicks on his payroll, it was. Seton Hall lost by 35.

Basketball is an easy game to fix. Players can boost an opponent's score simply by not playing tight defense. And defensive mistakes don't show up in the statistics. Or if something needs to be done on offense, a player on the take can always make a bad pass, throwing the ball out of bounds. Shots can be missed. Any variety of moves can pass for simple mistakes. As Jack Ramsay once explained, "Nobody can tell when a player is shaving points. Nobody!"

When the word about Seton Hall got out, I was playing the Eastern Regionals in Charlotte. Another of my high school friends, Jack Egan, was playing in the regionals for St. Joseph's. Jack, Al Senavitas, and I had all played on the same summer league team in high school. Both St. Joe's and Wake stayed in the same place, the Coliseum Motel in Charlotte, so Jack and I had time to talk about what had happened to Al's team. We both were concerned and said it must be tough on

Al. Wake Forest beat St. Bonaventure in the regional semifinals, but then we lost to St. Joe's in the finals, ending our season. Just a few weeks later, Jack and two other St. Joe's players were accused of being involved with the gamblers. I felt sick. Not only was he a good friend, but I thought about what the charges would do to him. And I was right to be worried. The incident destroyed his career. Jack Egan was a high-caliber player. He was 6'8", and he could run and shoot and jump. He would have been a cinch to go in the first round of the NBA draft. St. Joe's was coached by the great Jack Ramsay and had gone on to take third in the NCAA Final Four, beating Utah in the consolation game. Egan had been the main reason for their success and had been named to the Final Four all-tournament team.

Just days earlier, he had been talking to me about what a terrible thing the situation was for Seton Hall and how happy we were that Al Senavitas was not involved personally. Obviously, as Jack talked with me about Al, he must have been living under tremendous pressure, knowing the investigation was going on. Jack was married, with a baby on the way. There were bills to pay and other pressures. Then he and his teammates were charged. The news broke the morning before their team banquet. The banquet had to be changed completely. The guys involved didn't even attend. The NCAA put an asterisk beside their tournament wins in the record books, and the players' names were dropped from the records. If there had been a 10-man All-American team selected in those days, Jack Egan would have been on it. Without question, he was a true All-American. But he never played pro ball.

With the news of Jack and Seton Hall, the point-spread scandal began to hit home with me. First Al Senavitas had been tainted by his teammates. And then Egan, my summer league teammate and good friend, was directly involved. Later the investigation would spread to other schools, including North Carolina and NC State. Other guys I had played against there and had come to know would admit their involvement. Still, I was pretty naïve about the whole thing.

I had other things on my mind. We had a good team that year, and with almost everybody coming back, things looked good for us to have a great team the next year, my last.

The scandal didn't concern me again until later that spring when I was called into the basketball office. Charlie Bryant, one of Bones McKinney's assistant coaches, asked me if I knew anything about it. I told him I didn't, and we went on to talk about other things. I never thought any more about it until exam time. One day I was studying and sunbathing with some friends on the roof of a second-floor wing of my dorm, when two men dressed in suits stuck their heads out of the window of my room on the third floor. They yelled down and told me to get up there right away.

I was a cocky kind of guy and acted annoyed with the way they had yelled the order at me in front of my friends. So these two guys called down again and said that they had come to see me about a very serious matter. I went up to the room, and they identified themselves as being with the New York District Attorney's office. They said I should take a shower and come with them immediately to the office of the college president, Dr. Harold Tribble. I did what they said, but almost with arrogance. After I got my shower and quickly dressed, we walked across campus to Dr. Tribble's office. On the way, they said another Wake player and I were involved in the point-shaving scandal and were in serious trouble. I thought, "What the hell?" I knew I hadn't fixed any games. They didn't know what in the world they were talking about. Then I thought about Al's teammates at Seton Hall, and it hit me that someone on our team I didn't know about might be involved somehow.

That really made me mad. We had a good team. We beat Duke and Art Heyman and Jeff Mullins for the ACC championship that year. After that we beat St. John's, which had a great team, in Madison Square Garden. From there, we went to the regional finals in Charlotte. It was a long string of games from the ACC tournament to Madison Square Garden and then to the regionals. I felt that, if we had gotten a reasonable amount of rest, we would have made it to the

Final Four. The more I thought about it, the angrier I got. I figured someone on our team had screwed up some of our games.

As we walked across campus, the agents didn't identify the other player. I was dying to know. We got to Tribble's office, and I was still trying to figure out who had done something stupid. Then I realized it had to be me or Lennie Chappell, our All-American center. We were the only guys who had the ball, and if anybody was going to throw the game, it would be us. Then I thought, "There's no way Lennie would do something like that." He and I were too close. I would have known it. Somehow, it would have come up between us. Still, there was no one else it could be. The more I thought about it, the madder I got. "Just let me get ahold of Lennie in Tribble's office," I said to myself. I was ready for a confrontation.

Instead, Dr. Tribble met us outside his office. He excused us from the two guys from the DA's office and took me into a side room.

"Billy," he said, "I have to tell you that serious allegations have been made against you and a teammate. I want to ask you something, and I'll only ask you one time [I'll always respect him for that]. Are you guilty? Because if you are, tell me right now, and I'll do what I can to help you.

"If you're not, I also want you to tell me. And I'll do everything I can as president to get this straightened out as soon as possible without embarrassing you, your family, or the university."

I told him, "Dr. Tribble, I can assure you I've never been contacted by gamblers. I don't know what these guys are talking about."

Still no one had told me who the other player was. We went back into Dr. Tribble's office and waited with the two New York men for the other player to arrive. As I sat there, I got angry again, thinking that someone on the team had thrown some of our games and gotten me in trouble. I was about ready to jump up and punch out whoever walked through that door—which would have been suicide if it had been Lennie because he was 6'8" and weighed 240. Right away I was taking the position that the other player must be guilty. I knew I wasn't, but these two guys from the New York DA's office wouldn't come all the way to Carolina just for their health.

Then in walked Jackie Jensen, who is now a very successful coach at Guilford College. You have to understand something. Jack Jensen was a gym rat, a nonscholarship player. He was more of a sports fan than an athlete. He was very knowledgeable about basketball. He had always hung around the team, even in the off-season. He hadn't even made the team when he first came to school, but then he hitchhiked to Ohio once to see us play Ohio State. Bones McKinney heard about it and said that anybody who would hitchhike to Ohio to see us play should be on the team. So Bones gave him a uniform. Jackie never got into more than a couple of games.

There I was, all ready to fight, but when Jensen walked in the door, I busted out laughing. "You gotta be kidding me," I said. "Are we making a movie here, or is this a joke?"

I had kind of suspected that the whole thing might be some movie or something. The year before, when I was a sophomore, there were plans to shoot a movie on the Wake Forest campus starring Bing Crosby and Fabian. The Baptists (who ran the university) finally nixed the idea because part of the script called for Fabian to wind up in a girls' dorm. But the producers had planned for me to double for Fabian on the basketball court. Without the players knowing it, the movie crews actually shot some footage. We were playing Clemson and had run up a pretty good lead by halftime. So Bones left me on the bench for the second half. I was sitting there and brooding because Choppy Patterson from Clemson was challenging me as the top sophomore guard in the conference. I had played my ass off the first half and had outplayed him. But then I had to sit on the bench while he got to play and throw up his load the second half. I sat there angry the whole period until Bones called a time-out with a couple of minutes to go. Then he told me to go back into the game. He told the other four players to go to the baseline while I dribbled the ball outside.

"That's crazy," I said to myself. "What's he trying to do, embarrass Clemson?"

But I did what he said, and the Clemson players thought I was trying to embarrass them, so they came out and fouled the hell out of me. I made the shots, and Clemson took the ball down the floor but missed. We got the ball back, and again Bones had us do the same crazy thing. They were getting really mad and fouled me again. And again the pattern repeated itself. When Bones told us to run the play again, I got mad and told him it was crazy and I wasn't going to do it anymore.

After the game, Bones was furious with me. I asked him why in the world he wanted us to run that crazy play. Then he told me about the movie. They were shooting some footage and needed to create some action for Fabian. So you can imagine that when these government investigators came to my room the thought flashed through my mind: they're making another damn movie. And here was Jensen. I laughed out loud.

The guys from the DA's office looked annoyed. "Listen here, fella," one of them said, "you're in a lot of trouble."

I couldn't help smiling at the idea that Jensen could be involved in throwing a game. "Hey, you guys gotta be kidding me," I said.

They asked a few questions, and the blood left Jensen's face. He was scared to death. "I've only gotten to take a few shots," he said, "and I always try to make them." How could he throw a game? he asked. He never even knew when he would be getting to play. Even Dr. Tribble seemed kind of amused, as serious as the situation was. If the allegatons had been true, they could have destroyed basketball at Wake Forest.

Tribble reminded the investigators that we would have to weather this storm in the middle of exams.

The best way to weather it, one of them said, was for me to go to New York the next day to answer questions for the district attorney. To me, it was the perfect opportunity to get out of taking the tests. "I'll go to New York tomorrow and take makeup exams later," I said. I was excited. I could go to New York and have a little fun while setting these monkeys straight. And I would be getting out of exams. It would also give me a chance to drop by Philly to see my girl friend, Barbara (now my wife), who was then in nursing school.

The investigators agreed and left Dr. Tribble's office. Then he turned to us and said, "We've got to make sure the press doesn't get to this."

Jensen and I kind of laughed and said we didn't know anything about it anyway. At the time, I didn't know how serious the accusations were. I didn't realize that many people would come to believe I was involved. The investigation would eventually become very widespread, touching many of the major schools in the country. And everyone understood that it could have gone much further. Everyone seemed to realize: "If they can get to Jack Ramsay's kids, then they can get to anybody's kids." The investigation went around the country and probably could have gone into other schools, but the authorities seemed to get their fill of information, and the investigation stopped. You got the idea that they finally got who they were looking for in the inner level of the gambling ring, and after that the investigators let the whole thing drop.

The person the authorities were after was Jack Molinas. His is a sad story of wasted talent and intelligence. He had been a star at Columbia University in the 1950s. Then he moved on to the NBA, where he was a great performer for the Fort Wayne Pistons. But then he was caught gambling on his own team and was banished from the NBA. His basketball career gone, Molinas somehow went to law school. Supposedly a mature adult in his thirties, he couldn't leave gambling alone and began fixing college games. He used his big name and contacts and knowledge of the game to work inside some of the nation's best teams. He was the heart of the 1960s scandal. When the authorities finally caught him, they sent him to prison. He was later paroled, but died under suspicious circumstances, probably related to his gambling.

At the time, I didn't know this big picture. All I knew was

that these investigators had the wrong ideas. But I was going to get a free trip to New York out of it. After the meeting in Dr. Tribble's office, I went back to my room, and, man, I was really feeling high on the hog. I didn't have to cram for exams. I was going to New York, and later, I would maybe see my girl friend. I could take makeup exams later.

But before I could even appreciate it, Bones McKinney came up to my room and asked me to go to the house of Bill Gibson, the athletic director. Mr. Gibson was a former FBI agent, and when we got to his house, he and Bones started asking me if I really wanted to go to New York. They said it would be a long trip and I'd have to talk to people I didn't know. I began to wonder, "What are we going through all this for?" Then they brought in two investigators from the North Carolina State Bureau of Investigation, who started talking about granting me immunity from prosecution.

"Wait a minute," I said. "Why wouldn't I want to go to New York and straighten them out?" I didn't realize it at the time, but some people thought I was guilty. Not Bones. But I suspected that Gibson felt that way. I could see how people would view me that way. I was a guy who always had an angle going, always had ways to make cash. To them, I fit the type that would shave points.

Bones and Gibson said maybe I shouldn't go. But I was thickheaded and told them I was going. Then the SBI investigators got angry and gave the definite impression they thought I was guilty. When it was all over, I realized the investigators were maybe a little disappointed. It looked better for them to get me than the New York DA's office.

As arranged, I flew to Newark the next morning. There was nobody there to meet me. I didn't know what to do. I sat around awhile and started thinking this must be a joke or something. There wasn't even anybody at the airport. I waited a half hour or so and then went over to the ticket center to make reservations to return to Greensboro. Then I sat back down and waited for my return flight. I waited an hour or so, and then this guy comes up to me, opens his coat, and shows me a badge. It was almost like another movie scene. He said he was with the New York district attorney's office and told me to come with him. We got into a cop car and rode to New York. On the way, this guy got lost driving back to his own office. That really got to me.

"This guy can't even find police headquarters," I said to myself. "I can't wait to get in there and straighten these guys out." I felt it was important and I could get in there quickly, answer their questions, end this nonsense, and head back home.

We finally got to this police station, and inside it was like "Hill Street Blues." All kinds of stuff going on. The guy told me to have a seat. I waited there 40 minutes, and as I did, I saw different players coming and going: Hubie White from Villanova, Lou Brown from Carolina, Stan Niewierowski from NC State. They called me in to get my picture taken. Then they told me to sit down again. So it was another 40 minutes of watching the "Hill Street" scene in the station. All that time, I was getting really puffy and thinking how I was going to go right in and straighten these guys out.

I soon learned it wasn't going to be a simple matter. The main man of the investigation was Peter Andreoli. He worked for Frank Hogan, the New York district attorney who broke open the basketball scandals of the 1950s and '60s. The 1961 investigation began with rumors of gambling and game fixing at Madison Square Garden. Hogan had Andreoli and other investigators check out the rumors. They found they were true, and the investigation spread from there. By the time I was brought in, the investigators had begun shuttling suspected players in and out of interviews with Andreoli. The whole effort was aimed at getting at the people at the center of the ring, particularly Jack Molinas.

I walked in and sat down across the table from Andreoli. He had a surly attitude and threw a pack of about 15 to 20 pictures across the table to me and asked if I knew any of them. Thinking he was trying to trick me, I looked carefully. There were several black guys dressed in basketball uniforms, but I set them aside because there were no black basketball players in the South in those days. I looked at one white guy dressed in funny clothes, a real clown. I thought I might know him, but he wasn't familiar. I put them out on the table and looked them over again.

"Maybe I should recognize these, " I said, "but I really don't know them."

Andreoli gathered the pictures up, looked at me, and threw them down on the table.

"We know what kind of guy you are," he said angrily. "You're the kind of guy who thinks he's too goddamn smart to get caught."

Right away that shocked me into reality. It was not going to be easy to convince these people I was innocent. I realized I was going to have to be combative. That started my competitive juices to flowing.

Then he told me to go back outside and wait again. None of it made sense. I kept thinking it was just like in the movies. They were throwing pictures at me and screaming and hollering. There I was, a young kid with no legal counsel. It's staggering, now that I think about it, that the university sent me up there without a lawyer.

I waited another two and a half hours, and then another investigator came out and told me they had a room for me over at the Manhattan Hotel. He said they would call me in the morning when they were ready to see me.

I went to the hotel, where the other suspected players were staying. Then I grabbed some dinner and phoned my parents and told them some accusations had been made. My father was then the head coach at Lehigh University.

"I'm up here in a kind of crazy situation," I told them.

My dad asked me if I wanted him to come to New York to help.

"Nah," I said. "I'm fine." I admitted to being a little worried, but I felt confident that I could show the investigators they were making a mistake.

Then I phoned Bones. At that point, he was probably

somewhat on the fence as far as believing I was innocent.

"How's it going?" he asked.

"It's a pain," I said and explained how they were acting and interrogating me.

Bones blew up. "I'll tell you this," he shouted into the phone. "They'll not intimidate one of my players. I'm coming up there tomorrow to get the whole thing straight."

With that, the situation turned comical again. Bones was getting on his high horse.

"Coach, you don't have to come up here," I said. "I'll get it all straight."

"Are you sure?" he asked.

After I assured him and hung up the phone, I lay down, kind of laughing to myself about how silly the whole thing was. But when I thought of that Andreoli guy, I sobered up and started wondering if it was possible for them to make me guilty. Suppose I got steamrollered? What if somebody was trying to frame me? It started making me a little bit insecure. Damn. Suppose nobody believed me? What if I got kicked out of school? I was more than a little nervous. I couldn't wait until morning to try to get things straight.

The next day, I demanded to see the two investigators who had suggested I come to New York. They had been double-teaming me, as they do in investigations, one playing the tough guy, the other the nice guy. I told the nice guy I wanted an audience with Andreoli, and he got me one pretty quickly.

Andreoli started off by saying he knew I was involved and everyone would be better off if I admitted it and quit wasting their time. I said I wasn't guilty, so he started asking me questions again. Did I know Jack Molinas? I said I didn't know him, but I had heard his name from basketball. Then he asked me whom I had met with after the game against St. John's in Madison Square Garden. I said I hadn't met with anybody. My girl friend had come up for the game against New York University. I wondered if they were trying to get Barbara involved in this. That worried me. They kept asking me other questions, but after every two or three, they would ask me again whom I had met after the St. John's game. Allie Hart was my roommate on the road. He would know that I was in my room after the game.

Then they brought another guy in to question me about basketball. "How come you only scored five points against St. John's?" he asked.

Suddenly I felt comfortable. Now they were on my turf, talking about basketball. I felt some confidence. We had won by 20 points and had been expected to lose the game. The explanation of my scoring was a technical one. They were double-teaming and face-guarding me, making it tough for me to score. So Bones used me as a screen instead of a scorer. As a result, two of my teammates scored 60 points between them. With the answer, I felt real good. I thought I had made these guys look like fools. They didn't know anything about basketball. Still, they didn't act impressed with what I said. I was on a roller coaster.

They told me Bones had called and raised hell with them about intimidating me. They told me what a sorry individual I was to put my coach in a position of defending me when I was really guilty. The session went on for another hour or so, until lunch.

During the lunch break, I heard the news that Ray Paprocky, the great guard at New York University, was being called before the grand jury. That rattled me. I had played against Ray, and in that particular game, he had been the best guard. He had made an absolute fool of me, scoring 30 points or more. "Holy cow," I thought. "This guy is a great player. I hope he's not guilty." As it turned out, Ray *was* involved. He was another great player whose career was ruined. Years later, as a television commentator, I would go to New York to interview Ray, who had rebuilt his life despite everything. He had a fine family and a good career with the New York City Fire Department. When I interviewed him, he told me how a gambler came on to him as a sophomore. The gambler asked for $10 worth of tickets, and when Ray got them, the gambler paid him $100. Ray was married and his wife pregnant. He needed the money. "As I found out later, that was the come-on," Ray said. "And by my taking the $100, I guess I was hooked, insofar as it was going to go on and on and on, which it eventually did." His marriage and expected child made him "prime bait," Ray said. "I was relatively easy for them. And I had some soul searching to do, and eventually I decided that I was ready . . . I said that we couldn't win every game we played. And why not make some money on it?" Ray was just like a number of other young college kids across the country: naïve. At first the gamblers told him he just had to make the games close. "Don't worry about losing," they said. Later he learned it was much more serious than that.

As I ate lunch that day in the Manhattan, the scuttlebutt about the game was going around the place. I realized then that Paprocky and the others were just a small part of it. "This is a big widespread investigation," I thought, and it made me wonder who was guilty and who wasn't. I knew only one thing: I wasn't. And I felt I was getting framed up there. I was getting nothing accomplished. They didn't believe me. The more I talked, the more they were convinced I was a wise guy. So I called back to school and told coach I wanted to come back and take my exams. Bones and Tribble phoned the people in New York and told them, unless further discussions were necessary, to send me back home.

The investigators said it was a big mistake. "This kid's guilty. He's lying. It's a matter of time until we break him. It's not good for you to support him. He's near confessing." So Dr. Tribble phoned me again and asked me if I had given my very best answers. I said I had and that I wanted to come back. At the time I didn't realize it, but Wake Forest was doing more to support me than any other schools had done for their athletes.

Bones met me at the airport and drove me to Dr. Tribble's house to meet right away with the president. As we drove, Bones had me repeat the questions I was asked in New York. When I finished, he shook his head and said it still didn't make any sense.

At his house, Dr. Tribble informed me that the university

had to make a statement. "The people in New York feel you're guilty," he said. "I'm sticking by you. And the university accepts your word." At the time, perhaps I didn't realize it, but that was a tremendous amount of support. It was certainly counter to what the New York district attorney believed. He said flatly that I was involved. The North Carolina SBI believed that, too. Tribble put out a statement for the press, saying I had been to New York and answered questions for the district attorney. The university supported my claims of innocence, the statement said.

The story ran with my picture back in my hometown of Bethlehem. At that time, no one had been found innocent. People had to think I was guilty.

After the statement was released, Dr. Tribble turned back to the problem. He thought the most important thing was to get Jackie Jensen and me together to discuss it. "Did they ask you any questions about Jack?" he asked.

"None," I said.

He said Jack and I should come to his office tomorrow to hash this thing out. Dr. Tribble's support was comforting. But I still felt nervous. These guys in New York seemed wacko. "They're never gonna believe me," I said.

The next day we met, and Tribble said he assumed Jack would soon have to go to New York. The mention of that worried Jack. He was the type of guy who would cut off his arm before he would hurt Wake Forest basketball. We started going through the questions again, concentrating on the main one: Who had come to see me after the game in New York?

Jack looked at me and asked, "Don't you remember? You brought your friend to my room."

Then it hit me. They were talking about Dick Markowitz from George Washington University. Allie, my roommate, and I had been asleep at about 2 A.M. when Dick came up to my room. He was 6'5" or 6'6", dark-complected, and that night he was wearing a real sharp suit and a hat. I later realized he resembled Jack Molinas.

Dickie Markowitz was from Allentown, Pennsylvania. I

had met him in high school through basketball, and we had hung around together some because we were from the same area. That night there had been a triple-header at the Garden, and George Washington had lost. Afterward, the coach put his team on the bus and went home. But Dick had missed the bus, so he came to my room in the Manhattan. He banged on the door in the middle of the night and asked me for a place to sleep. There weren't any extra beds in our room. But I realized Jensen was the only guy on the team without a road roommate. I had taken Markowitz to Jensen's room that night. As I said, Markowitz looked an awful lot like Molinas. By then, the investigation had gotten pretty deep. The DA's office was watching the key players with a stakeout at the hotel. The stakeout must have seen Markowitz come to my room and assumed it was Molinas.

"No wonder they think I'm lying," I said.

Tribble said he would call the New York investigators immediately. He did, and the investigators contacted Dick and confirmed the story. Basically, that ended it, although they never acknowledged my innocence.

Years later, I went back and interviewed Andreoli. He talked long about the investigation, but he didn't even remember questioning me. It was like I was a nothing in the total scope of the probe.

I hadn't seen Dick Markowitz since the night he came to my room in 1961, until a few years ago. I was in Los Angeles, broadcasting a UCLA game. In my motel room, I got a phone call.

"Let's go to the Erving Street Park and get a game of three-on-three going," this voice said. "You used to like to play three-on-three."

"I can still shoot," I said. "I just can't run. Who is this?"

It was Markowitz. He was in the real estate business in Long Beach. I met him for lunch the next day.

"Remember the time you had the police investigate me?" he asked.

I laughed and explained the whole story.

"What made me nervous," he said after I had finished, "was

that when I got back to my room after they questioned me, I pulled back the covers to get in bed and found a $100 bill. I didn't know where it came from. I thought, 'Holy cow, Packer is getting me in real trouble!' I kept it and never told anyone."

Once the investigators confirmed it was Markowitz who came to my room that night, the story ended for me. Wake Forest never made another statement about the investigation. The people in New York sent no follow-up to the school confirming that I was cleared. The investigation went on. The University of North Carolina and NC State were disciplined, with a reduction in the number of basketball scholarships they could offer. And the number of games they could play was cut back. The university presidents decided there was too much emphasis on basketball and shut down the Dixie Classic, the great early season tournament held in North Carolina each year.

Twenty years later, it's easy to laugh about some of what happened. But point scandals are still a threat today. In 1961, most people didn't remember what happened in 1951. And, of course, another gambling scandal erupted at Boston College in 1981 and then again at Tulane this past year. It's inevitable that it will happen again. People are always trying to get an edge by gambling. There's always that situation. Always a new breed of kids coming along who don't know the dangers. Until it's touched your family, you can't understand what it would be like.

That's why I decided to dredge up an old story.

CHAPTER

3

TALKING THE GAME

For me, basketball and broadcasting made a natural combination. Being a color man is just an extension of playing, coaching, recruiting and living basketball. For me, that's where it all began. First, my father was a coach. And as a coach's son, I was the quintessential gym rat. Always shooting. Always dribbling. A kid playing a game with a ball half his size. And along with all that, there was that natural extra ingredient. I could talk. Even as a youngster, I was good on my feet. Almost from the start, my favorite subject was basketball. With my father being the coach, I had plenty of opportunities to talk the game. In school, I became a class officer and got my first real taste of public speaking. I guess you could say that sealed my fate.

When I got to college, I was fortunate to be coached by a guy who was terrific on his feet, Horace Albert "Bones" McKinney. A skinny 6'6" kid out of Durham, North Carolina, he earned his reputation everywhere he went. Bones played two years at NC State before his college career was interrupted by World War II. He went into the army, played some ball, and then came out and switched to the University of North Carolina, playing on the 1946 team that made it all the way to the NCAA finals. From there, he had some wild times playing for Washington in the NBA, where he was All-Pro in 1947 and '49. By the time I got to Wake Forest in 1959, Bones had converted to Southern Baptism, completed seminary, and become a Baptist preacher. Besides being a minister, he was one of the most entertaining speakers in the region. He hasn't gained a national reputation, but I have yet to hear or see anyone better than Bones.

At Wake Forest, I kind of fell in with him off the court as his driver and public-speaking partner. We traveled around a lot together during my college years, mostly talking at Baptist churches and civic groups. Sometimes Bones would come to my dorm room at an odd hour, unannounced, and take me off to drive for him. He's a terrible driver, so he used to like to have someone go along with him.

The trips were all pretty much alike. He always liked to stop for Pepsis and Nabs and Moon Pies. He ate those things while we rode, no matter whether it was before or after supper. We'd haul down the road to some out-of-the-way little Baptist church somewhere, and Bones would go in there and turn the people on their ears. Everyone, including Bones, would laugh and holler and talk together. Then I'd get up and speak a little bit, even though I was a Catholic. After that, Bones and I would joke and raise hell down the road going back to college. Those trips with Bones were an important part of my background. They gave me the chance to speak and feel very comfortable about voicing my opinions.

Bones, of course, gets a kick out of my saying that. He never noticed my being reluctant to express myself. In fact, he once told Smith Barrier, the North Carolina newspaper sports editor, "I played Packer all the time so I wouldn't have to listen to him on the bench. He really didn't talk that much, but he always had suggestions."

Only a coach like Bones could handle that. He was very good in establishing a give-and-take rapport with his players. Even during close games, he gave us the opportunity to discuss what the team should be doing. Sometimes that got to be quite a problem. I'll never forget our 1962 NCAA tournament game against Yale in the Palestra in Philadelphia. We had watched Yale practice the day before and were very unimpressed with their talent. As a matter of fact, we couldn't really concentrate on the Yale game because we were thinking down the road to other games. Unfortunately, their talent was a lot better than it looked in warm-ups, and they played a very spirited game. With seconds left to go, the score was tied. We got the ball out of bounds about 60 feet from the basket. Bones called a time-out and gave us a hell of a lecture about running the clock out and getting them into overtime. Then, he said, we could play the way we knew how to play and beat them there.

"You guys have really screwed this up," he said. "And you almost blew your chance to move on in the NCAA tournament. Just get the ball in bounds to Packer and let him run the clock out. Then we'll use the five minutes in overtime to blow them out of here."

I interrupted to tell him that I didn't think that was a good idea at all. I said that I thought I could throw a pass to our center, Len Chappell. Yale had nobody tall enough to defend against him. I said I could throw the pass right at the rim, although it was 60 feet away, and when Lenny caught the ball, someone would foul him. Then at least we would have a chance to go to the foul line with two seconds remaining. If Lenny made the fouls, we'd win the game, I said. "Let's take a shot at it."

Bones looked at us a second in the huddle and said that wasn't a bad idea. "Let's try it," he decided finally. "If you think you can do it."

Sure I thought I could do it. After the time-out, we set up so I could throw the long pass. The referee standing under the basket at the other end of the court was a guy by the name of Steve Honzo. He was a friend from my hometown area. Steve was a great referee. He was very fair and firm and knew the game. The play is one of those memories that remains vivid. I recall confidently throwing the pass, watching it in the air, and getting the feeling that it was good. I knew I had done my job. So my eyes didn't focus on anything other than Lenny downcourt. And when I looked at Lenny, I also saw Steve Honzo standing just behind him, clear as day. As the ball was coming, Lenny pushed the Yale player, a guy by the name of Shumacker. The whistle blew, and my whole plan came crashing down. Instead of completing the perfect pass I had talked Bones into using, we were going to be beaten in the opening rounds of the NCAA tournament by Yale, a team we had laughed at in practice the day before. Sure enough, Steve Honzo, as good an official as he was, instead of saying, "Let's just let this game go into overtime. Let's pretend I didn't see it," called a foul on Chappell. So we walked to the foul line at the other end of the floor. Bones called a time-out before the shot. I remember walking across the floor—it seemed like 50 miles—to face up to the preacher waiting at the bench. As expected, he had a few things to say about my idea. Bones ripped my rear end, saying something like, if the guy made those shots, I would be walking back to Winston-Salem from Philadelphia. I never felt so bad in my whole life.

This poor Shumacker turned out to be a very good student and a nice guy but a horrible foul shooter. He went to the line and crossed himself, and Bones immediately called a time-out to let the guy think about the shot.

A Reverend Hollingsworth, a Baptist minister, always traveled with our team and sat on the bench. During the time-out, Bones called Hollingsworth over.

"Did you see what that boy did on the foul line?" Bones asked the preacher. Hollingsworth said he hadn't noticed.

"He crossed himself," Bones said seriously. "Now we're gonna find out who's right and who's wrong, the Catholics or the Baptists."

Just to make sure Shumacker was good and iced up for the shots, Bones let him go to the line again and then called a second time-out. The ball was probably 250 pounds in Shumacker's hands by the time he finally got to shoot. It bounced off the rim, and Yale rebounded but missed again. The game went into overtime. We won there and moved on, eventually making the Final Four. I learned a good lesson about how costly ideas and opinions can be. And Bones, of course, kept his faith.

That wasn't the first time in my career that I got my comeuppance from a coach, and it certainly wouldn't be the last. Over the years, as a player, then as an assistant coach, and finally as a broadcaster, I had the pleasure—and sometimes the humiliation—of running into some of the best coaches in college basketball. Each of them taught me a valuable lesson. Collectively, they reinforced the lesson I'd learned from Bones: Never try to second-guess a coach.

There's never been a classier coach in the history of basketball than Frank McGuire. He led St. John's to the 1952 NCAA championship game and then won the National Championship with his North Carolina team in 1957. After that, he went down to South Carolina and put together a great program. He had the Gamecocks ranked number one in the nation for a good part of the 1970 season. When I was a player, I held him in awe. Then, when I became an assistant coach at Wake Forest, I found out just how incredibly tough a competitor he was.

One night, in 1969, Wake played down in South Carolina against his team, which included John Roche and Tom Owens. Frank McGuire planned for Roche to freeze the ball. Roche was to go down into the corner near the end of each half and put his back to the defense and dribble the ball until he was ready to make his move. It was very difficult to defense. That particular year, a rule had been passed treating the corner just like the mid-court area. If you dribbled or held the ball in that area and were closely guarded for more than five seconds, the officials would call a jump ball. We had instructed our players to be prepared for that situation. If Roche moved down into the corner, our players were to guard him closely to create the jump ball. It was the first time we played South Carolina that year, and the officials didn't acknowledge our strategy. They wouldn't call for a jump ball.

Lou Bello was refereeing the game that night, and I was screaming at him, "Lou, that's a jump ball!" Just seconds before the half ended, he turned to me and said, "What are you talking about?"

After the buzzer, I went up to Lou and said, "This is a six-foot radius from the corner. It's a closely guarded situation." Suddenly, as we were talking, I was knocked off to the side. I looked around to see what had hit me. Coach McGuire had come down and given me a good shove and knocked me out of the way. My first instinct was to smack him. Then I realized, "Hey, there are 14,000 people from South Carolina here. Coach McGuire is the king." Also, he might have been able to whip me.

In McGuire's mind, I had no business out there as an assistant coach talking to a referee. He may have been right. I'll never forget trying to get back to the locker room. The police came and got me out of the way. Then the police left me, and I was escorted by two pretty good-size guys from South Carolina who I knew were not fans of mine. We came to the basket supports, and the path narrowed so that only one person could go through at a time. I thought, "Uh-oh, when we walk through this little path here, there's going to be room for only one guy. And that's going to be me." Otherwise, I figured I'd be lying on the floor after these two guys walloped me. Just as we got to the basket support, I was able to throw a little quick elbow in the direction of both of these guys and put them down on the side. Quickly, I weaseled my way into the dressing room to safety.

I didn't have any problem getting out for the second half because there were plenty of police around to protect me. I eventually got a nice apology from the ACC's head of officials through a memorandum he put out to all officials about the rule. A few years later, when I saw Coach McGuire, he acknowledged the incident and said he was glad to see I was on top of my game. He's always been a great credit to basketball.

While an assistant coach at Wake Forest, I also had the

opportunity to work with Neil Johnston, who had once been one of the great players in the history of the NBA. He went to Ohio State but left school to become a professional baseball player. Out of the need for additional income for his new family, he decided to try out for the Philadelphia Warriors. Neil was a 6'9" rawboned individual, who developed a superb hook shot. Without question, he was one of the great competitors ever to play in professional sports. He led the NBA in scoring and rebounding for three years in the early fifties. Undoubtedly, Neil was one of the best centers ever to play. Unfortunately, Neil died a few years ago while playing basketball in the backyard with his sons.

We became good friends while we worked at Wake. He was a very proud man, and rightfully so. One day I pulled a prank, one of those smart-aleck moves that make you feel worse about them as they progress. I had been home for lunch, reading *Sports Illustrated,* and found an article about Bill Russell. The piece contained comments by Red Auerbach about what a great player Russell was. Auerbach mentioned that when Bill Russell joined the league he quickly dominated other inside players, so much so that he essentially forced some of them out of the game. Neil was among those mentioned. I thought I would kid Neil a little bit about that, and when I returned from lunch that day, I said, "Gee, Neil, they've got an article about you in *Sports Illustrated,* and I thought it was a little unfair."

I thought I'd get his goat a little bit, so I paraphrased the article and told him, "Russell ran you out of the league." Neil took great offense at that. I was wrong for not realizing how proud Neil was about his abilities; it was just a bonehead move on my part. That very afternoon, Neil initiated a lawsuit against Red Auerbach and *Sports Illustrated* for those comments.

By the time practice had started at three o'clock, he had come back and was obviously very, very angry. He charged that Auerbach and the magazine had ruined his reputation as a player and his potential reputation as a coach by suggesting that he was a quitter, which he certainly was not.

The situation got way out of hand and was one of those times when I wished I had kept my mouth shut. The suit eventually went nowhere, as suits of that nature usually do. But it did create a good deal of agony for a person I considered a close friend.

While Neil Johnston ran a heated battle with the media, John Thompson merely conducts a cold war. He does it without apologies, without doubt. That leads a lot of people to write about what a dictator, what an intimidator he is. Well, I think he's totally misunderstood, and many people underestimate his great coaching ability. I consider him a friend and a very knowledgeable person, not only about basketball but about life in general. He has been kind enough in recent years, when CBS is doing a Georgetown basketball game on TV, to let us come in and watch his team practice. To understand what a privilege that is, you have to know that John holds his practices sacred. He views himself as a teacher and the practice session as his classroom. He has been criticized by many people for not having open practice. But John is unique, and I think a coach has the right and the need to run his program uniquely. I don't think any outsider has the right to ask him to change.

Still, as a network analyst working with play-by-play men like Gary Bender and Brent Musburger, I realize it's important to have the opportunity to watch a team practice, to examine the players, to recognize their faces and their styles, to build background on the team before the broadcast. John has been kind enough to recognize that and has let us into practice. Our appearance is always well orchestrated, down to when we come, when we leave, what we do, where we sit. Controlling and isolating the elements in the game, in practice, is very important to John Thompson. And when broadcasters visit his practice, they are an element to be controlled. Again, in John's program, that's a positive, not a negative, factor.

During the 1984–85 season, I went to Georgetown to do a game and took my son, Mark, with me. Of course, when

Mark's on a trip with me, he travels anywhere I go, so I never thought about whether he would be allowed into Georgetown's practice. We appeared at the gym at exactly 6:30, as we were told. We were led into practice and found two chairs waiting for us against the wall, about 60 feet from the court. There were three people: Gary Bender, Mark, and me. Mark stood up while Gary and I sat down and began observing practice. John was running his drills and so forth in a very orderly fashion, when suddenly he turned around and looked at me and said, "Who is that fella?" John was standing about 150 feet away, so I hollered back, "That's my son, Mark."

Without batting an eyelash, he looked back at me and said, "*My* son doesn't get in to see Georgetown practice." No more had to be said. I got the point and took it very well: John had invited Gary and me to the practice. We had a job to do, and he had a job to do. The next time I needed to see one of his practices, I should ask permission for my son to be there. And if I don't, it should be accepted as a fact that he is not invited. I respect John for that kind of discipline. Of course, it sometimes gets him in a little public relations trouble. But that's part of John's system. He believes in it strongly, which, in my opinion, is the unique ingredient in all successful coaches. They find what works for them, and they stick with it. The coach has to believe in it so strongly that he's able to convince his players to believe in it. Certainly strategy matters. But the most important factor is that the coach believes in his system, no matter what it is. And John Thompson sure believes in his discipline.

When it comes to discipline, I don't suppose there's ever been a truly great basketball player who doesn't have it. However, there are different philosophies about it. Take Bill Russell, for example. Russell is something of a mystery character. I can't imagine his playing records ever being challenged. His great leadership on the court, his presence, is set in basketball history. I've had the opportunity to meet him on several occasions. At first he seems to be very reserved. But when he warms up, he tells stories that are spellbinding, particularly those about Red Auerbach. Russell, it seems, hated to practice. Most of the time, he knew what he needed to do to keep in condition, mentally and physically. That attitude ran contrary to the approach of Red Auerbach, who ran excellent practices and had his team prepared to play at all times. Bill said that part of Auerbach's genius was his ability to know what he could get out of a player and how to get the best. One day, the team arrived at practice and found Red sitting at center court with a number of cigars laid out in front of him. He said, "Guys, I've got enough cigars to stay here all day long. So we're going to stay here until you put out the way I want you to put out."

When Bill saw all of those cigars there, he realized that Red was planning to make a full day of it. So, instead of going half-speed, Russell decided to go all-out. And when Bill Russell decided to go full-speed, as he did in games, he destroyed the practice. Russell just intimidated everyone to the point that nothing got done. Finally, Auerbach realized there was no need to go any further with the practice. Russell had made it impossible.

I can't imagine Red Auerbach letting up on anyone in practice. But he learned not to worry about Bill Russell's practicing. He decided the best thing to do was to make sure that Russell was prepared for the ball games and to leave practice for his less accomplished players. Auerbach proved that he was versatile in handling individual players. Instead of being thickheaded and demanding, he put together a flexible team concept of the best kind. It won championships. championships.

There are few coaches who, like Auerbach, can be said to have made a permanent imprint on the sport of basketball. Dean Smith is one. His record at the University of North Carolina is reaching legendary proportions. He's one of the most complete coaches in the game, combining every phase of the job—promotions, recruiting, bench coaching, game preparation, innovative court strategy, long-term relationships with his players—for a first-rate package. I often admire how calculated he is in handling himself and his program on and off the court. His first year as head coach was my senior year in college, so I've had an opportunity to watch his development. It's hard to conceive that he was hung in effigy his second or third year at the University of North Carolina. Realizing that, you have to compliment the key administrative people who didn't listen to the students and the disgruntled supporters. The administration backed him, and Dean has repaid their support in gold. It would be hard to imagine anyone duplicating his record.

If anything, Dean's years at Carolina have been marked by his control, over his program and over himself. Dean normally has things buttoned up so tight there is little or no opportunity for mistake. Even when things don't go well for him, he responds with control. Only once over the many years, the many games, have I ever seen him lose that control, and in a way it was nice to see that happen, to know that he's human. Everybody has those days when he isn't on top of his game. With Dean Smith, I've only seen that happen once, and that was back in 1975.

Wake Forest was playing Carolina in Chapel Hill. Marvin "Skeeter" Francis, an ACC administrative official, was in charge of calling the television time-outs during the game. Skeeter was also the former sports information director at Wake Forest. During that broadcast, Skeeter called a television time-out right when Wake Forest needed it badly. Now, Skeeter didn't control when television time-outs were called. He simply followed the established procedure, and Dean Smith certainly would have recognized that if he hadn't been emotionally involved in the game. When the game ended and Wake Forest won, Dean really jumped on Skeeter. As the postgame press conference began, Dean essentially accused Skeeter of using the television time-outs to help Wake win the game. In more than 20 years of watching Dean Smith, it was the only time I've seen him respond emotionally rather than logically.

Over the years of watching dozens and dozens of coaches, one thing has become clear: there are no magic charms, no mystical tricks to building a winning team. Only hard work, discipline, clear goals, and a lot of heart will get you there. And no one displayed these characteristics better than John Wooden.

As a young assistant coach, I badly wanted to learn the perfect answer for becoming a supersuccessful head coach. Coach Wooden was obviously the best in the United States, and I felt that, if I could watch him in action, maybe I would find the key to success. I learned that Wooden attended only one camp each year, at Campbell College in Carolina, now called Campbell University. I got in contact with some people Bones had known at Campbell for years and was able to get a job there as a first-year staffer. The people at Campbell didn't know how badly I wanted to be housed in the same dormitory as Coach Wooden, where I figured I could learn a lot by observing everything he did, from how he disciplined himself in a daily routine to the instructional methods he used. With Campbell College in Buie's Creek, North Carolina, having high summer temperatures, I assumed that Coach Wooden would be assigned to the film room, where he would have air conditioning all day long and could avoid the strenuous court sessions. Even in those days, Campbell had become one of the largest camps in the country and would bus the kids to gyms in nearby communities. Each head coach and assistant would have a gym, where the players would be drilled in certain skills. I went down for orientation on Sunday afternoon, and Coach Wooden was there. Press Maravich helped me get into the dormitory where he and Coach Wooden were staying. Although Press and Wooden were extreme opposites in the way they acted, they were close friends.

Once I had my rooming assignment, I really didn't care which skill gym I worked. I was assigned to lay-up drills and individual moves with Tee Frey, a longtime staffer at Campbell and a head coach at Oak Ridge Academy. He was a wonderful guy and had been a great baseball player in his day. Wooden asked to take the toughest and most boring assignment of all, individual defense, where intensity and a great deal of movement were needed. I was surprised that he was willing to take on such a tough job, because this was just a summer camp.

Throughout those two weeks, I observed Wooden so closely that I stopped seeing him as a basketball giant. In fact, if he hadn't already won four or five National Championships, I would have had a hard time believing it. He was almost beyond belief. His conversations on basketball in our little living room in our dorm suite were usually so basic that I would go back to my room wondering if he was telling the truth. His comments were elementary, some of the same things that I'd been taught back in junior high, and I often wondered when he would get into the heavy material. Every day, Coach would be the first guy up and the first guy to bed. After he would get into his pajamas and call it a night at about 10 o'clock, the other fellows would break out the cards and the games, which were kept out of view as long as Coach was awake. It was almost like he was the grandfather, and they waited for him to go to bed so the kids could play.

During those two weeks, I really never had a one-on-one conversation with him until one day when we were all invited to go to Fred McCall's home for a staff dinner. Fred, head basketball coach and athletic director at Campbell, had a daughter who was heading off for her first year at the University of North Carolina, and these were during the "burn, baby, burn" days of student protests of Vietnam and of marijuana on college campuses. Although the decade had taken a while to get to campuses in the South, when it arrived, it brought with it a great tide of unrest. So conversation centered on Fred McCall's daughter's going into that atmosphere. Coach Wooden said, "Well, fortunately because of her upbringing and her Christian parents and the attitude she had at home, she should have no trouble making the adjustment."

I had taken about all of that conversation that I could handle and had always been somewhat outspoken, so I interrupted Coach Wooden to say that I didn't believe that that was the only thing that would prevent Fred's daughter from having problems and adjusting at Carolina. Her home-town was far from the environment she would encounter at North Carolina. I thought that, despite the upbringing she had, there would still be that question of her adjustment. Coach Wooden disagreed, but allowed me to have my opinion. Even though the discussion had nothing to do with basket-ball, the other coaches there looked at me like "Billy, you have to be crazy to take a position other than Coach Wood-en's." I thought it funny that they esteemed him so much that none of them wanted to disagree with him, even if it was about something like child rearing.

When the two weeks were over, I had accomplished every-thing I wanted to at Campbell College as far as working with kids and fellow coaches went. But I remember on my drive back to Winston-Salem still being totally confused as to just who this Coach Wooden was. The whole philosophy that had brought him National Championships seemed based on sim-plicity and repetition. By the time I got home, I realized that there was no magic secret to becoming a head coach and that there were probably a lot of different ways to skin a cat. Coach Wooden had simply found the way that was successful for him. He seemed to be saying that the real key to being successful in coaching or anything is to go ahead and be yourself, do the things you believe in, and work hard at reaching your goals. That seems simple enough.

As a player, I had always enjoyed visiting the campuses of the schools we played against. Clemson was one of the most fun places to visit during my years at Wake Forest, particu-larly because of the Tigers' colorful coach, Press Maravich.

The only thing annoying about Clemson was that Press had a little son who used to hang around the gym all the time while we practiced. He was just a little over four feet, small for his age, and very skinny. But he could really handle the ball—so well, in fact, that he was really kind of a wise guy. He would constantly come up and say how his dad's team was going to beat us the next night in the ball game. While we were trying to shoot around, he would sneak in to steal the ball, just being a total pain in the neck. The boy kept aggravating me to the point that I said, "Kid, it's a shame that you'll never get a chance to play college basketball because you're going to be so damn small that the game of basketball is going to go right by you."

He was in the fifth or sixth grade then. Well, the next time I saw him, he was a senior in high school in Raleigh, North Carolina, playing in the state high school all-star game. I believe he scored 45 points in the game. By then, he had grown to be about 6'5" and weighed about 140 pounds. There were many of us who said then, "Gee it's a shame the kid can't put on some weight. Maybe he'd be a decent college player."

Of course, Pete Maravich became the greatest scorer and player in LSU history and the leading scorer in the history of collegiate basketball, averaging 44.2 points per game over his college career, or a point a minute each game. If nothing else, I've learned not to pass judgment too quickly on skinny little kids.

Fortunately for my ego, I'm not the only one who makes that type of mistake. Bones McKinney probably remembers with some chagrin this story about "the big one that got away."

It happened during the spring of my junior year in college. In the off-season, the players at Wake Forest would gather for pickup games. One day, we had just finished a real knock-down, drag-out game and had gone outside to sit on the ledge by the gym for a break. As we talked, a man drove up with his son, a high school kid about 6'5", 175 pounds, a young-looking kid. The father introduced himself to Bones and said, "This is my son here. He's an outstanding player from New Jersey and would really like to come to Wake Forest."

Bones really didn't pay him too much attention other than to be cordial. He looked over at a player on our team, Al Koehler, who was a real hard-nosed backcourt player from New Jersey. "Well, fella," Bones said to the father, "why don't we go upstairs, and I'll let Al play against him. We'll see how he looks."

Koehler had played tough defense against Duke's Art

Heyman, the national player of the year, so it wasn't like Al couldn't guard somebody. Al was just a little too strong and mature for this young player. He worked him over pretty well. Afterward, it seemed quite obvious to Bones that this young man would have a difficult time playing at the ACC's level of competition. Bones told the father that Wake Forest wasn't the place for the boy, that maybe he would be better off looking at a lower level of competiton, and that, certainly, the son should put on some weight.

A few years later, after I had become Bones's assistant coach, I came across a letter from the father who had brought his son down to Wake Forest. The father said he appreciated Bones taking the time to let the boy work out. He assured Bones the boy would grow and become a lot stronger. In effect, the father said, "I know he's going to become a great player, and I'd really appreciate your reconsidering and giving him a chance to come to Wake Forest."

Bones wrote back a short note thanking the father for the correspondence, indicating that, maybe a little bit down the road, he'd take another look at the kid. Somehow that never worked out. The kid eventually ended up going to the University of Miami, where he did a fair job, making All-American and leading the nation in scoring. He went on to become one of the great forwards in the history of the NBA. His name? Rick Barry. Maybe Bones misjudged that one.

But then again, recruiting isn't an easy business. Right after college, I had the chance to find out firsthand how tough a recruiter's job can be.

Very few people, through the course of their lives, get the opportunity to do the things they would really like to do. I've been fortunate that most of the right career opportunities have fallen into place for me. When I first got out of college, I wanted to be involved in business and was given the chance. I felt that my career there would have progressed nicely. But in the back of my mind was always that thrill of being involved in coaching. I knew I didn't want to be a coach my entire adult life, but I wanted to try it for a while. I set a tight time schedule for my coaching experience. I thought four years would have to be set aside for being an assistant coach, working toward getting a head coaching position at a school where I felt I could win, while running a clean, consistent program. If something broke in less than four years, fine, but without question I would commit to assistant coaching for four years, then reevaluate whether I was capable of being a college head coach and whether the opportunity was there. If the opportunity wasn't, I decided I would get out of coaching, no matter how much I enjoyed it, and get back into business.

My coaching days began with Bones McKinney asking me to help him recruit Herm Gilliam, a black player in Winston-Salem. In the mid-sixties, a black athlete had not entered the Atlantic Coast Conference. Integration was something I had never thought about that much. Segregation was just an accepted practice in the South, and I had never been one to concern myself with racial matters one way or another.

Then Bones decided to recruit Herm Gilliam. If he could get Herm to commit to Wake Forest, and if Herm could get in academically, Bones would be the first to break the color line. He had talked a few years before of recruiting Lou Hudson from Greensboro, but didn't proceed with it at the time. Hudson, of course, went to the University of Minnesota and became an All-American there and had a great career in the NBA. That had to leave an impression on a lot of ACC coaches. In the case of Herm, Bones didn't worry that he was going to be the first to recruit a black athlete in the Atlantic Coast Conference.

I had never seen Herm Gilliam and had never really been involved in recruiting anybody. As a player at Wake, I had talked to recruits who had visited the school. So after graduation, I took this request from Bones as a real challenge and responsibility. It also gave me the chance to stay close to basketball. I went to see Herm play, and he was obviously a very talented player, a real clean-cut kid. I knew the first time I met him that he would be a real important part of anybody's program, on and off the court. Herm's mother was a schoolteacher. I got to be very close to Herm and thought a great deal of him. I spent time with him and talked with him about coming to Wake Forest. He became very interested and decided to pursue his collegiate career at Wake Forest. His high school coach was a sharp fellow who realized what the challenges would be to Herm off and on the court in being the first black athlete to attend an ACC school. Herm's coach, George Green, questioned me closely and gave me the opportunity to express my opinions. The experience impressed upon me that the only way to be successful in recruiting was to be honest. That meant long-term success as opposed to a quick hit. I really came to appreciate the coach as a person looking after Herm's best interest.

There was only one problem. Herm had excellent grades at Adkins High School, but in those days the ACC required an absolute minimum combined score of 800 on the Scholastic Aptitude Test for an athlete to be eligible for a scholarship to an Atlantic Coast Conference school. Many people felt that the rule had been imposed to keep black athletes out of ACC schools, but I never thought that was the reason. Herm's college board scores were not 800, but they were certainly within striking distance. So I told Herm, if he wanted to go to Wake Forest, I'd make a program where he could study a preparatory course for college boards. I was sure he would meet the entrance requirements with that course.

He decided that was what he wanted to do, and I arranged the course. That spring and early summer, until he took the college boards, he worked diligently, getting ready for the test. But then, one day, I realized that if Herm didn't get the 800, I would have put him at a terrible disadvantage for college. Obviously, he could play for anybody in the United States, and I thought that, if he didn't make the 800, he should have plans to go somewhere else. We talked about it, and he decided that if he didn't get in to Wake Forest, Purdue was the school he would like to attend. He had a relative in the area up there, and the Big 10 had always been a good place for black athletes from the South. Walter Bellamy, Lou Hudson, and Carl Eller had all attended college in the Big 10. I told Herm I had a friend at Purdue in the economics department who might help and that I would contact the coaching staff for help.

So I called my friend at Purdue, Zeno Martin, who was in close with the Athletic Department and had been doing some tutoring. I asked Zeno to get in touch with one of the basketball coaches so Herm would have a place to go if he didn't qualify for the ACC. I was put in contact with one of the assistant coaches, Bob King, one of the highest-caliber people I met in coaching. I told Bob about Herm and explained he was a great player who could help any program in the United States. I said I'd be shocked if Herm wouldn't be in the starting lineup for any college in the country and that I was recruiting him for Wake Forest. I explained the situation and asked Bob not to worry about recruiting him. Bob King is the kind of person who gave me his word that he would not interfere with Herm's attempt to boost his college boards and that Purdue would assure Herm a scholarship if he did not make the 800.

The day Herm's college board scores came back was one of the saddest days I ever had in collegiate athletics. He came up shy about 10 points of making the 800. There were no exceptions in those days. If you had the 800, you were in. If you had 799, you were out. I met with Herm and his mother and explained that he did not have the 800. Herm suggested that he could maybe go to prep school. "Maybe I could try again," he said.

I told Herm that really wasn't the deal. "We assured Purdue that you would go there, and it'll be a great place for you." He agreed. I called Bob King, who had been a man of his word. He had not interfered with Herm that entire summer, yet the scholarship was waiting. Herm went to Purdue and was in the starting lineup his sophomore year. He became an All-Big-10 player, helped lead the Boilermakers to the Final Four, later enjoyed a fine pro career, and is an outstanding young man today. Again the ACC's loss was the Big 10's gain.

The experience told me that I needed to make the commitment to become an assistant coach for Bones McKinney. I signed up and had a terrific experience over the next five years.

My first responsibility at Wake Forest was recruiting. Bones really hadn't had anybody get on the road for him for a couple of years, so I had mapped out what I thought would be a good strategy. Knowing that so many players from the Northeast had been successful in the Atlantic Coast Conference, I planned to work New York, New Jersey, and Pennsylvania, all in three weeks. My wife and I were both from Bethlehem, Pennsylvania, which was centrally located for working those three states. I took Barbara home to visit with her family, and then set out on the trail. The first assignment was New York City. I figured if there was going to be any one place where there would be great players, certainly it would be there, especially since no one in the ACC had recruited black players. Bones and I had no hesitance about being the first coaches to recruit a black athlete into the ACC.

My first day in New York was interesting. I had never spent much time in New York, and no time recruiting, but the one school that I and everybody else had heard of was Power Memorial. Lew Alcindor (Kareem Abdul-Jabbar), of course, had just graduated from there, and the high school was recognized around the country as having one of the leading basketball teams. I figured there was no better place to start than there. I went into the school that day and talked with the guidance counselor about some of the athletes they had returning that year. Norwood Todmann's name was mentioned immediately. An excellent outside shooter with fine grades, he was expected to be the leading scorer the next year. Power was an excellent school, and Tod looked to be the kind of kid we wanted.

I asked around if anybody knew where I could meet with him during the summer or where I could see him play, and quite surprisingly one of the fellows in the office said Tod would be playing that night for a coach named Mike Tynberg. I had never heard of Mike Tynberg then, but he later became a good friend and one of the gurus of high school basketball in New York City, along with Howie Garfinkle. Being naïve about the recruiting trail, I just assumed that Mike was coaching a regular playground team. When I asked where I could meet Mike, they gave me a phone number. I called Mike, and he said his team was going to be playing and Tod was on it. Why didn't I meet them under the clock on 42nd Street and 8th Avenue? I said no problem, but I had no idea what "under the clock" meant.

We were to meet at about 5:30 that evening, so I got down there at about 5:00 and looked around, pretending I knew what I was doing. Not long after I got there, I noticed some kids standing around on the corner eating hot dogs. I figured they had to be players, although I couldn't believe their size. One big, strong white kid was 6'11", and another was about 6'7", a perfectly built power forward type. I went over and introduced myself and asked if any of them had heard of Mike Tynberg. They said he was the coach of their team and they were waiting for him. I thought, "Gee, in addition to Norwood Todmann, this is going to be some kind of team I'm going to see. It must be some kind of playground league."

It wasn't long before Mike showed up. He was a middle-aged guy about 5'8" and didn't look much like a coach, no whistle with him or anything. But he was a nice guy and welcomed me to come along as the team caught a bus to go over to Newark and play a local team there. I thought this must be some kind of league to go all the way out of town to play. We rode over, and on the way Mike told me what a great team he had, what outstanding players, the works. I thought he was kind of pumping a little smoke there at me. I had no idea of the caliber of the ball team I was riding over to Newark with on the bus. At the playground, the guys took their gym bags into this little recreational center and changed in the men's room. It wasn't a very professional operation; they all had on cheap outfits, shirts and all different kinds of pants. I sat down and waited to see my first summer league play. Mike's guys were relatively young, rising juniors and seniors in high school. The guys on the Newark team were older, at least college age and some even older. It was interesting to watch them shoot around. Without question, they had some excellent talent, and I wondered how these high school kids were ever going to compete against them. I didn't know these Newark fellows, but they obviously could play. When Mike's team came out for lay-up drills, the first kid dribbled in and dunked two-handed, backward over the top of his head. I almost fell off the bleachers. I couldn't believe there was someone who had that kind of talent. Then I saw that all these kids could stuff without any problem, and they were all gifted ball handlers. I thought, "Hey, if this is what basketball is like in New York City, then this team could go down as a unit and play very favorably in the Atlantic Coast Conference." I couldn't believe the talent.

Later I found out just what a rookie I was. My "discovery" was already on the minds of the major coaches across the country and had been for quite some time. The kid who dunked that one over the top of his head was Dean Meminger, who later became an All-American star for Al McGuire at Marquette. The big white kid was Bob Linehart, who still holds all the rebounding records at the University of Georgia. The big power forward was Jim McMillan, who became an All-American at Columbia and then went on to have a great pro career. That night I was witness to what was the finest collection of rising junior and senior talent in all of New York City. And Mike Tynberg turned out to be more than just a coach of a summer league team. Year after year, he was the assembler of some of the great talent in New York City. I was just fortunate enough on my first night in New York to stumble right into the heart of the hottest action. It was quite a disappointment for me to realize that this wasn't a regular summer league team and that New York wasn't filled with kids just like the ones on that team. The group I witnessed would turn out to be some of the best players in collegiate basketball.

Still, my trip was anything but a failure. I got off on the right foot with Mike Tynberg and apparently with Norwood Todmann because I was able to recruit Norwood for Wake

Forest that next year. He was the first major player out of New York ever to be recruited to Wake Forest. The next year, he was followed by one of his close friends, Charlie Davis, whom Norwood helped us recruit. Charlie, of course, turned out to be an outstanding All-American player for Wake Forest. That night in New York proved to be a fine education for a rookie recruiter on his first trip out.

As awkward as it was, the job of recruiter was priceless in that over the years it provided me with a ticket to see some of the top talent in basketball. Like Robert McAdoo.

McAdoo, one of the outstanding players in the history of the state of North Carolina, was somewhat of a late bloomer. When I was recruiting him for Wake Forest, Robert had a very unorthodox shot, one he keeps to this day. Another big player in North Carolina at the time was Danny Trailer, a 7-footer from Winston-Salem. Robert was about 6'10" and from Greensboro. They played in the same league and went head to head against one another. Everybody was heavily recruiting Danny Trailer, but not too many coaches were after Robert. His grades were adequate, but he had spent more time as a youngster with musical instruments, playing in the band, than he had playing basketball. When I saw his unusual shot for the first time he seemed rather uncoordinated. But the more I watched him play, the more I came to realize what a great talent he was. It was obvious he loved to play basketball.

Robert took up high-jumping on the track team his senior year in high school. He never really had any formal training but selected as his technique the Fosbury Flip, which television had popularized that year. Without any real instruction, Robert perfected the flip on his own. That spring, the Junior Olympics were held at Wake Forest, and Robert came over to participate in the high jump. His main competition was Bobby Jones, who was just a junior then but still an outstanding basketball player and high-jumper. Bobby had perfected his technique in both basketball and track and field and was the man to beat. I took Bobby and Robert to lunch that day, and although they knew of each other, they weren't good friends at the time. They eventually became teammates at the University of North Carolina and later played against each other for many years in the NBA. At that time Bobby was considered the top high-jumper in the state.

When the high jump competition began after lunch, Robert and I decided to sit up on the bank around the track and watch. Robert had on an old pair of blue jeans, old Converse sneakers, and a sweatshirt. Bobby Jones had three or four pairs of track shoes and nice sweat suits and really looked the part of the young trackster. Throughout the early competition, McAdoo just sat there with me. When the high jump reached 6′4″, I got a little nervous and said, "Robert, I understand the high jump's up to 6′4″. When are you going to go down there?"

"Well," he said, "I think I'll join in at about 6′5″ or so and make my jump at that time."

A few minutes later, he strolled on down to the jump area, and I wondered where his track equipment was. Well, his track equipment was what he had on. He had shorts and a T-shirt under his jeans and sweatshirt, but instead of track shoes, he kept on the beat-up sneakers. He got into the high jump competition with Bobby Jones, and they went at it head to head, some of the best high-jumping done in North Carolina. Robert eventually won the event on fewer misses, although they tied at the same height, a little over 6′9″, I believe. I was amazed that Robert was able to do so well without the formal training and proper equipment, and I wondered what height he could have turned in if he had had the training and equipment. Both kids were actually great athletes, but I was prouder of Robert and what he had accomplished under the circumstances.

By winning the event, he qualified for the National Junior Olympics that were to be held in California later that summer. I got a call from him when the time approached for him to go to the Olympics. I had been keeping up with Robert pretty closely. He said he wanted to come over to Wake Forest and play basketball that day. And I said, "Robert, aren't you going to the Junior Olympics?"

He said he didn't think it was right for him to go to the Junior Olympics because he had to pay for his bus trip to meet up with those other qualifiers in Knoxville, Tennessee. He felt that, since he qualified as leading jumper, he really shouldn't have to pay his own way to get out to Tennessee.

"I certainly couldn't agree with you more," I said. "But I hate to see you miss out on an opportunity like this. I'm sure I could help you get the bus fare if that's the problem."

No, he said, it was more the point that a champion ought to get the opportunity to go to the event without having to pay his own way there. I admired Robert for his attitude and also for the fact that he was able to abide by principle and not worry about the potential glory that could come from winning the national high jump event. Bobby Jones went on in place of Robert to Tennessee and then on to the national championship. He actually won the national championship in high jump but did not beat the record Robert had set back in the qualifying round in the state of North Carolina. It's kind of amazing that they became close friends and teammates at Carolina. Considering all they have accomplished in the course of their basketball careers now, I look back at that afternoon and think what a great thrill it was to watch two high school champions go after each other in such clean, hard-fought competition.

Only by being a recruiter was I able to witness first-hand the development of such a great player. And while I didn't know it at the time, I was broadening my background as a broadcaster. I would soon understand that such experiences would be priceless.

CHAPTER

4

BREAKIN' IN

In itself, my broadcasting career is nothing unusual, except for one thing. It has paralleled the rise of televised college basketball. Over the course of my broadcasting years, the game has become a hot TV item. At times, the growth has been a little too fast. But the overall effect has been good. It's a great game, and TV makes it accessible to a broad range of people. Over the past two decades, I've had something of an inside view of the transformation of basketball from a cozy little game into big-time network entertainment. It's a fascinating story, featuring some real characters. Eddie Einhorn, C. D. Chesley, Dick Enberg, Al McGuire. Not to mention the cast of thousands—the coaches, players, and officials.

For me, basketball and broadcasting make a natural combination. Even at a young age, I was able to get on my feet and talk. I always enjoyed that. I was a class officer in school and was always around athletics. With my father being a coach, there were plenty of opportunities for me to learn how to converse with people, especially about basketball.

Even though I had never been a star player, my playing

and coaching experiences had given me a pretty strong background in basketball, and my assistant coach job actually led to my eventual career in broadcasting.

In 1969, I was working for Jack McCloskey at Wake Forest as an assistant coach when I got my first chance to go on the air. The radio station broadcasting the Wake Forest games wanted to have a postgame coach interview. This shows just how much the game has changed. Today the coaches get paid big money to do these radio game shows. But back then, in the 1960s, there was seldom any money for that, and coaches didn't want to do them because it was an imposition on their time. The odds were better that an assistant coach would do the shows. So the people broadcasting the team games approached me about a postgame interview. "You have nothing to do when the game is over," they said. "And you're an assistant coach. Why don't you come on the air and give us a little five-minute recap of what happened in the game?"

"Sure," I said.

I did my first show after we played Duke in Durham. Duke had had a great program and was our chief rival. We had an upstart team at Wake, where McCloskey was building the program. The game went down to the line, and we had several chances to win it in regulation. Then we had more opportunities in overtime, with one-and-one foul shots. But for some reason, we just couldn't cash in. Duke made the free throws and won it. So, when I went up for the interview, I was hot and wasn't thinking of being a professional broadcaster. I said what I felt: "When you get a rival in the position to beat them, that's the time you tighten up your jockstrap and make those foul shots." That's exactly the way I said it. Of course, the Wake Forest radio network went crazy. Here was a Baptist school with an assistant coach talking about jockstraps on the air. The repercussions the next morning were strong. The gist of the message was "Hey, Billy, the way you said things wasn't good. Your enthusiasm was great, but you can't say 'tighten up your jockstrap' on the Wake Forest radio network."

Wake Forest didn't even have beer advertisers on the air

during those days. But the funny thing about it was that, while my remark brought very negative responses from the administration, the school, and the Deacon Club boosters, it was a hit with the radio audience. People said, "This guy Packer is refreshing. He's saying something." So, despite the initial problem, the postgame interview became a regular feature. When the games ended, I would go on the air and talk about what had happened. I enjoyed it and never really thought much about its being my first broadcasting experience.

I left coaching in 1970 and went into the radio business as a partner and general sales manager in a North Carolina station, WAIR. Immediately, my partners and I had to think of additional ways we could create sales. We decided broadcasting high school football made business sense. I did the on-air work so we wouldn't have to pay talent fees. During the day, I would go out and sell ads, and at night I'd broadcast.

I'll never forget the first game we did. I didn't know there was any such thing as a rights fee or that you even had to tell someone you were coming to broadcast. We decided our first game would be at East Forsyth High School. I showed up at the game with our equipment although I didn't even know how to hook it up, where it went, or anything else about it. Still, I felt proud because we had all the advertising spots sold out. I was pretty sure things would work out.

The first trouble came when I went out to get the equipment hooked up. I ran into Fred Lewis, the principal, whom I'd known for quite a long time, and said, "Fred, where do I go to hook up my equipment?"

He looked at me funny and asked, "For what?"

"For the game. We're going to broadcast your game."

He said, "Nobody called me about it."

"Why do we call you?" I asked.

"Well, I'm the principal. You've got to get the rights to broadcast this game."

"Aw, I didn't know anything about that. Gee, I'm sorry. The next time we come, I'll be sure to do that. Now, where do you hook up?"

"I told you," he said, "you have to get permission to broadcast this game, and next time maybe you'll have the courtesy to call me in advance. You'll not broadcast this game tonight."

Oh, I was angry. We had lost the $250 in sales and couldn't broadcast the game. It wasn't so much the ego deflation of not being able to broadcast as much as the loss of sales revenue. That hurt. But after I thought about it, I admired Lewis for doing it. It taught me a lesson, one that I carry with me to this day, especially in handling major network things. When they go to a college campus, I think networks have the tendency to say, "Hey, here we are. Get out of the way." It doesn't matter where you go or who you are: you shouldn't have that attitude. I'll never forget Lewis. It was his game, his facility, his people, his team, and his fans, and I owed him the courtesy of getting permission to broadcast.

I don't think I've ever abused my broadcasting privilege since. And there have been times, because of our position with the national network, when a broadcast team could do almost anything it wanted. College administrators seem to have the attitude that "we'd better not make those network guys angry because they're paying big bucks."

There were other funny little lessons to learn from broadcasting high school games. One night, after I had a couple of years of experience, I went to West Forsyth High School to air a game. The broadcast booth was nothing more than four telegraph poles and a four-by-eight sheet of plywood nailed to the top of them. The object was to climb the pole and sit about eight feet above the fans to broadcast. Well, that particular day was nice, with temperatures in the 60s, even after I got out there to set up for the game. But it was one of those weird fall days when the temperatures fall 30 degrees between the time the sun goes down and eight o'clock at night. I was wearing just a sweater and was absolutely freezing up there announcing this game. Two friends of mine, two of my closest friends in Winston, showed up at halftime.

They start hollering at me while I was up on this plywood

atop the poles, "You gettin' cold up there?" I said, "Hey, guys, get me a coat or something." They just laughed and said, "You only have one more half to go. You don't need a coat." So I sat up there, finishing the game just shivering. I thought I was going to have pneumonia. They just waited and laughed. I couldn't figure out why they were staying for this high school game. When the game ended, they hollered to me, "Come on, let's go get something to eat." I said, "Fine, let me get my equipment." I got everything together and shimmied down the pole. When I got on the ground I said, "What are you guys doing out here?"

Well, my partner in the radio station had asked them to stop by to tell me the telephone lines went out and the station couldn't carry the game because there was no connection. They were supposed to tell me that nobody was hearing the game except me. I had frozen my tail off for nothing. That was another little part of my informal training, a little study in not being a hotshot. You can't think you're a big deal just because you're sitting on top of things, broadcasting the game.

As time passed, I became more professional, at least on a local basis. That's not to say things always went smoothly, though. One night, I was supposed to broadcast the state play-offs with Gail Henley, who did the play-by-play. Unfortunately, nobody notified Gail. I guess he just assumed that, when the regular season ended, he was through. Well, I got to the game and was setting up the equipment, when my son Mark, who was about ten, asked me, "Where is Gail?" I said, "He's probably down on the field, gathering information." I knew all the players, so I didn't bring any information about the game with me. I wasn't concerned. I hooked up the equipment and called the station to make sure everything sounded OK, and by the time I got back to the booth, Mark was really worried. "I don't see Gail down on the field anywhere," he said. "I don't know where he is."

I wasn't worried, but just in case, I called Gail's house to see if something had happened to him. Lo and behold, he picked up the phone. I said, "What the hell?" I knew he lived about 45 minutes from the stadium. "What are you doing home?"

"What do you mean," he said.

I told him we were supposed to be announcing the game, and he said he didn't know anything about it. So here I was. I didn't have a pencil or pen. No pad. No stopwatch. No game program. I didn't have any idea who the guys were on the other team. I had to figure out what to do. So I ran back to the booth, and there was no one around except my son, so I told him, "You start talking on this microphone so that they can hear you back at the radio station. Say anything you want. Talk about the people, how the marching band is in blue and green, or whatever you want to say. I've got to go round up some equipment."

I went down to the field where I saw a guy I knew who had a watch with a second hand. I borrowed the watch and then bummed a pencil from one of the newspaper reporters. Then I went up to the other broadcast booth and pretended to socialize with a broadcaster from the other team, High Point. While I sat there, I read his notes to steal some information. When I got back to our booth, Mark still thought that Gail was on his way. He didn't realize that he and I were doing the game. When he realized what we were going to do, he turned green.

And we did it. We went on the air, and I broadcast the game until Gail showed up. That taught me about preparation. You can never go to a game thinking that it's all going to work out. I don't take notes with me to games very often anymore. But I go prepared, and regardless of what could happen, I think I have the ability to carry a broadcast without any trouble. Preparation is the only thing that separates a good broadcaster from a bad one or a great one from an average one. The great ones are always well prepared, and that's the bottom line. The bad ones are the guys who have all the technical qualities, but they don't prepare to do the game and don't have enough knowledge and depth of information to carry it through. They just bull their way through games.

That particular year, the '71-'72 season, I began doing televised basketball games. There was no big plan for Billy Packer to become one of the broadcasters of ACC basketball. I kind of came in through the back door. Dick Andrews from Pilot Life Insurance had heard my comments after the Wake games and remembered me. Pilot Life had sponsored the early Atlantic Coast Conference television broadcasts produced by C. D. Chesley, the "father of televised ACC basketball." Chesley was putting together broadcast deals in the Philadelphia area in 1957 when Frank McGuire's undefeated North Carolina team came there to play in the NCAA regionals. Chesley produced a regional broadcast of the tournament games for several Carolina stations, and when the Tar Heels went on to the Final Four in Kansas City, Chesley and his associates quickly arranged to have the games broadcast back in Carolina. Recognizing a good thing, he spent the next several years nuturing the ACC's television coverage into strong regional entertainment, all of which only helped to strengthen the league.

By the time I came on the scene, ACC televised basketball was a thriving regional entity. When some of the big-name broadcasters couldn't appear, someone mentioned my name as a substitute. That's how I got my break on the air.

I considered it a great challenge. I had had just a taste of radio broadcasting but had never done anything on television. But just like any other well-informed fan, I thought I could handle it.

A funny thing happened, though. My first game was a mid-January contest between NC State and Maryland. Lefty Driesell won the game, and afterward, the producer sent me down on the floor to interview him. I had known Lefty for a long time. I had even played against him in the first game he ever coached, so I felt very comfortable with him.

I had never done any kind of postgame interview. I had been interviewed, but I was never the guy on the other end. The producer just assumed that I was a professional broadcaster, able to go down and do this interview. So I went down there and talked to Lefty just like I'd talk to him on the street.

I said, "Lefty, people think you're not much of a coach, but you coached a great game tonight."

People seemed to find it refreshing that someone would finally get on the air and say that kind of stuff. But the next day, I got a call from Clarence "Bighouse" Gaines, the legendary coach at Winston-Salem State, a guy I consider a good friend. He told me, almost like a father would, "Billy, you don't ever embarrass somebody like that. Lefty really handled it well, but the way you asked that question made it look like you were acting superior to him, as if you were putting him down. Don't ever do that again." That always stuck with me. There's a way to ask the question you want without embarrassing the person on the other end.

When I headed home to Winston-Salem that night after my first game, I was still on a high, even though it was close to midnight. The trip from Raleigh back to my home was about 85 miles, and I spent the whole time dreaming of things to come. For the first half hour of the ride home, I thought about the thrill of broadcasting, being involved in the game, having the best seat in the house, people bringing you Cokes at halftime, nobody disturbing you, and being able to say whatever came to mind during the course of the game. What a thrill. By the time I got to about Greensboro—about 60 miles—I decided that, not only did I enjoy broadcasting, but I thought I was pretty good at it. By the time I was almost home, I had arrived at the position that I was *great* at it.

When I pulled into my driveway, the bedroom light was on. I thought maybe the kids had been sick or something because it was about two in the morning. I went into the bedroom, and my wife Barbara was waiting up for me.

"I was just looking forward to talking to you," she said.

I asked her if she watched the game.

"I thought you were OK," she said.

"OK?!" I said. "You've got to be kidding! I'm really good at it!" We sat there and laughed awhile about my reaction and talked about some of the things that happened in the game. I could detect a trace of concern about this new thing I was doing. Finally, I said, "Barb, I'll tell you what. There's no way

I'm going to be able to continue this broadcasting and carry on a regular job and have the house all disrupted. I promise I'll quit doing it as soon as I've had a chance to do the national championships and the Olympics."

I felt good about my first broadcast, except for one thing. When you do one game, you want to do more. Still, I really didn't want to commit myself right away—assuming they even wanted me—because I was going out of town and I was afraid they might ask me to do a game that weekend. In my radio sales job, I had just won a trip to Hawaii for my wife and me. I sure as hell didn't want to say no to Chesley, but on the other hand, I didn't want to miss the trip. I was euphoric but nervous.

The whole time in Hawaii, I was thinking, "I wonder if Chesley is trying to get in touch with me." I sure hoped that one game wasn't my one shot at television. At that time, I didn't know very well what kind of producer Chesley was. Would he write official letters or give me formal notification of broadcasts or what? I didn't even know if I got paid. I never even asked. It wasn't important. Never in the whole time I worked with Chesley did I have a contract with him. He was a very informal person. When we got back from Hawaii a week later, I got a call from him, and he asked, "Where the hell you been?"

I told him I'd been out of town on business, and he said, "Well, I've been looking for you. I want you to do some more games for me." I breathed a sigh of relief.

I did all the games from then on. We never did discuss how much I would get paid, and I wasn't even concerned about it. I think I eventually got about $125 a game. But that was immaterial.

As far as I know, no one really had a formal arrangement with Chesley. Each year the season would end with the ACC tournament, and that would be it. A whole year would go by, and you'd never hear from him. He would disappear into the Carolina mountains, and that was the end of it.

This would happen every year I ever worked for him. Suddenly it was December, and he'd call, maybe a week before the first game, and he'd say, "Hey, kid, you going to be in Durham Saturday night? See you there." That was the extent of the relationship I had with him. I would never say, "Well now, Ches, are you going to pay me more this year?" or "Do you know what games I'm working?" or even "What time do you want me there." He just assumed that you knew, if there was a game at eight o'clock, you had to be there on time. And I'd be there, and it would all work out somehow.

Chesley was a genius at putting deals together with the schools. With that genius, he built ACC basketball into a unique entertainment package that gave the conference distinction. He also had a knack for finding employees dedicated to the product. His broadcast directors were big-time people, but his camera people and technicians were just kids from the University of North Carolina, which has a fine journalism school with radio and television programs. These weren't big union people with topflight credentials, but through dedication and intensity they produced some fine broadcasts.

Still, around every broadcast, even in the networks, there hovers the feeling that whatever can go wrong will go wrong. The 1971 ACC championship game between North Carolina and South Carolina is a good example. South Carolina's coach, Frank McGuire, had something of a chip on his shoulder. The other members of the league had voted against granting eligibility to one of his best athletes, Mike Grosso. And McGuire's departure from North Carolina under the cloud of the point-shaving scandal of 1961 probably left him with some resentment.

In those days, Chesley bought TV time by the hour. There was seldom an extended pregame or postgame show. Basically, they just showed the game—except during a championship game, when there was a postgame celebration with the winning coach and team.

Well, the 1971 finals came right down to the wire. North Carolina appeared to be in control, but there was a tap, and South Carolina's 6'3" Kevin Joyce beat North Carolina's 6'10" Lee Dedmon on the tap, Tom Owens drove to the basket, and laid it in to give the Gamecocks the championship. Well, the game ended right on the hour, and Chesley saw no reason to purchase another hour just for the celebration. Instead, the broadcast cut to the evening news. McGuire felt snubbed and claimed that the broadcast had been cut off out of spite. He felt the Big Four schools from Carolina—North Carolina, NC State, Wake Forest, and Duke—were involved in snubbing him. Actually, the schools had nothing to do with it. It had been strictly a business decision by Ches not to buy extra time.

Still, enough of a stink was raised that the next year Chesley decided to make sure he purchased ample time, an extra half hour. Unfortunately for Ches, but interestingly for me, the 1972 championship and celebration went by very quickly. We had covered everything there was to cover: the Most Valuable Player award and trophy presentation, the cutting of the nets, everything. And we still had a half hour to fill. The crowd had gone, and I ended up interviewing the guy that was sweeping out the Greensboro Coliseum about his thoughts on the game. We went off the air with a spotlight on the guy sweeping the floor.

No matter how much broadcasting experience I felt I was getting in those early years, it seemed there was always another lesson to learn, a new problem to be solved.

For one, I found out that there comes a time when you tend to get lax, and all of a sudden you draw a blank. I'm sure it's happened to each and every one of you. Maybe you've been out to dinner someplace, and you go to introduce a couple of people in your guest party, people you may know as well as you know your husband or wife, and all of a sudden you draw a blank. That can also happen to you in broadcasting, where being properly prepared, with your notes and research, can get you over those hurdles where your mind leaves you totally blank. And no matter how embarrassing a lapse can be at a dinner party, it's multiplied a thousand times when you go blank in front of a TV audience.

When I worked for C. D. Chesley, he always required me to go down on the floor and announce the starting lineup. I would give the name of each player, the class he was in, his hometown and position. This was never any problem for me, especially since the games were all ACC games. I knew the players as well as I knew the members of my own family.

Unfortunately, one night my mind just drew a blank when I was up at College Park, Maryland, doing a game involving the University of Maryland. The first player I introduced in the lineup was John Lucas. I'd known John for quite some time, even when he was back in high school, and I brought John out with "Starting in the first guard position is John Lucas, six foot three, a junior from Durham, North Carolina, playing guard from the University of Maryland." As John ran out on the court, I looked over to the sidelines, and standing over there was his running mate, Mo Howard. Lucas and he had been starting guards at the University of Maryland for two years, but for some reason, I just could not think of Mo's name. I looked over at John as he ran by me and said, "John, who's going to be playing in the backcourt with you?"

To this day, John probably doesn't realize the reason for the question, but he just laughed, turned around, and said, "Moe, of course." At that very instant, the name Moe rang a bell, and I was able to pick up the introduction without missing a beat: "and in the other guard position, six-foot-three-inch guard Moe Howard!" Nobody in the audience, television or live, realized that, if it had not been for John Lucas's comment, I never would have been able to think of Moe Howard's name.

From that day on, even though I could have named the players backward and forward, as well as their statistics, hometowns, and the like, I never went to center court to make an announcement about teams without having a card in my hand that had all that information on it. In subsequent years, I don't think I ever had to look at the card, but just knowing that I had it in my hand was my security blanket.

Before my second year of ACC broadcasting, Ches encouraged me to try for some postseason games with the network. He helped me arrange a meeting with a CBS official in New York to discuss doing the NIT. I'll never forget going in there. It shows just how the sport has changed. I met with Bill Fitts, a vice president of CBS. Since Chesley had set up the appointment, I was thinking maybe I'd really get a chance to do a national game. I went into Fitts's office and sat down. Not only did the fellow not know me; he didn't seem concerned over who I was. That really didn't bother me so much, but he started off his questioning with "Oh, yeah, you're the guy from that conference that has that ridiculous postseason tournament."

I said, "Well, I work in the ACC, and first of all, it's not ridiculous. The postseason tournament is something that's going to be the coming thing around the country. You'll find that other conferences will eventually attempt to copy what the ACC is doing."

I got into a heated argument with Bill. He started off telling me he had only a couple of minutes to talk. Right then I realized I wasn't going to get any job. We ended up in a spirited discussion that lasted about 45 minutes. I realized he wouldn't consider me to do the NIT. But I got one thing out of the meeting. I realized the people in New York making the decisions didn't have any special understanding of basketball marketing for television. In fact, their knowledge of the game and where it was going was certainly not superior to mine. The people putting together the ACC broadcasts saw things the people in New York didn't begin to understand.

My chance to do a big game didn't come until 1973, when Chesley went after national syndication by packaging a Super Bowl Sunday game between Maryland and NC State. Suddenly, I had my first chance to work before a nationwide audience. It was David Thompson's sophomore season at State. I worked the game with Ray Scott, a premier sports annoucer with a great command of broadcasting, the voice of the Green Bay Packers through much of their championship reign. I considered him and NBC's Curt Gowdy to be the crème de la crème of broadcasting in those days. This was quite a thrill for me. Hell, I'd never been in on something like this before.

I didn't get a chance to meet Scott the night before, so the morning of the game I was eager to see him. We had breakfast at a nearby Howard Johnson's. I'll never forget it. I thought the guy would be all together, a super pro. Maybe his valet would be bringing in his clothes or something like that. He came in with this old beat-up duffle bag. I was shocked. I never thought the guy would be carrying his own bag. But the thing that really shocked me was his blue shirt. Chesley's broadcast team used blue chroma key, which is a sheet set up behind the announcers used for filtering colors to provide a background. You couldn't wear blue shirts because the chroma key was blue.

I thought, "Holy cripe, I must have really screwed up. Chesley's probably using a different-color chroma key today, and here I am with the wrong color shirt on. I'm going to have to find another shirt." I was very shaken up thinking about that during breakfast. We finished, and he carried this goofy little bag over to the game with him.

During the rehearsal, the camera guy comes up to him and says, "Ray, you can't wear a blue shirt. We've got the blue chroma key."

And Ray says, "Oh, hell, I forgot all about it."

He takes off his shirt right there and reaches down into his duffle bag and pulls out an old brown, wrinkled-up shirt and puts it on.

Then Ray says, "You know, Billy, this is the only basketball game I'll do all year. I don't really keep up with it that much. I've heard a lot about you. Chesley tells me you're a really up-and-coming guy."

He's really making me feel good, saying all these nice things. Then he adds, "So you know I'm counting on you to run this broadcast. You tell it like you always do. I'll just hang in there. As the game goes on, I'll get into it. We'll have some fun with it."

I thought he was just saying that to relax me. I've never

been nervous announcing a game. But this was a national game, and whatever Ray Scott said, I was hanging on every word. The technicians called us about three minutes before game time. We stood at courtside, ready for the opening. Ray asked me, "Do you get nervous before a game?"

"No," I said, "I never get nervous."

"My palms get a little sweaty before a game," he said.

I was startled. Here was a guy who had done all the big broadcasts in sports. No one, perhaps other than Curt Gowdy, had a bigger reputation. I thought, "What is he doing getting nervous?"

"I've got to tell you about Jack Kemp," he said. "Kemp was brought on to help us broadcast the Super Bowl. Boy, he was just a quality guy. He had retired from football but hadn't gotten into politics yet. All week long before the game, Jack was on the field with all the players. He had tremendous rapport and everything worked out great. Everything he said was terrific. Then we got ready to go on the air the day of the game, and I looked over. Jack just froze up. He couldn't even talk. He said his lips were dry, and we had to get him off the set and calm him down. He couldn't go on the air."

Here was Ray Scott telling me this, and I'm thinking, "This is national TV. Is there a moment that comes that freezes you up and you can't do it?"

We went on the air, and I wondered what he was talking about. There was nothing different about national television. The game began, and I was off and flying. Ray opened up the game basically by saying, "I'm happy to be here at Maryland today with my buddy Billy Packer. He knows this game backward and forward, and I'm just going to sit back and watch and have some fun with you people today. Billy will tell us what's going on, and he'll keep us informed." And that was it. When he said that earlier, I thought he was just trying to make me feel good. But that was the tone for the broadcast. David Thompson won the game at the buzzer for State, and I had a great time doing the game. This national broadcast thing wasn't as big a deal as I thought it was. And big names like Ray Scott were real people, a pleasure to work with.

Before the start of the next season, 1973–74, there was talk of a nationally televised game on ABC between NC State and UCLA. I tried to get Ches to help me get on the air to broadcast it, but I never got anywhere. Bill Russell and Keith Jackson did the game for ABC. They had already been selected, and it was probably presumptuous on my part to think that I would have a chance. But at the end of the season, I got my first chance to work an NCAA tournament game for NBC, the Eastern Regionals game between State and Providence in Reynolds Coliseum on the State campus.

Actually, the game was a package deal between NBC and Eddie Einhorn's production company, TVS. It was the game when David Thompson leaped high on an alley-oop play and crashed to the floor, landing on his head. Everyone thought he was dead. Despite the fall, the game was great. State beat the Friars 92–78, starting Norm Sloan's team on the drive to the national championship.

The game was extremely physical. The referees had been moved in from other regions, and frankly, I don't believe they had ever seen the type of talent that was on the floor that game. With the leaping ability of David Thompson and Marvin Barnes, the game really got away from the officials. As things got more and more ragged, NC State took the advantage. Thompson was killing Providence with his patented jump shot from the deep corner. He took one of his shots and was hit on the arm, resulting in an air ball. It was an obvious foul that wasn't called. Instead, Providence started a break the other way.

David was very annoyed and looked back at the trailing referee as if to say, "Hey, you've got to be kidding." David was a polite, heads-up kid, not the type to ever say much of anything to anybody. But he was so annoyed that Providence got the break that he took off to chase the other nine players down court. When he got to the top of the key, a Providence player took a jump shot from the corner. David must have decided that, whether they called goaltending or not, he was going to get a piece of the ball. He took off at the foul line and went up so high it was frightening, as if he was suspended in air. Then his heel hit the shoulder of another player, turning David upside down in midair. He dropped head first onto the hardwood. His body was in a heap; his arms were bent grotesquely underneath his back. I thought he had died, that he had been killed instantly from the impact with the floor. It was almost as if someone had dropped him straight down from 10 feet up in the air onto his head. An eerie hush descended on the gymnasium. It was something I'd never sensed before in any sport. They brought out a stretcher and took him off the court.

Then, late in the second half, a hush came over the stadium. Something was happening down at one end of the arena. Thompson had come back onto the court. He had his head wrapped in a great white bandage and walked slowly to the end of the State bench and sat down. I couldn't believe it. The crowd was overjoyed to see him even walking.

I talked to him right after the game, and he was still completely in a daze. Only someone of his athletic ability could have survived that fall. Fortunately for NC State, David not only survived it but was able to go against UCLA the following week in a very memorable game in Greensboro. State upset UCLA and went on to win the national championship against Al McGuire's Marquette team.

The season and the tournament made me all the more thankful that I had a front row seat for some of the greatest moments in basketball.

CHAPTER
5
NETWORK DAYS

The next year, 1974–75, brought my first break with a network. When the ACC tournament was over, I got a call from Scotty Connal, who was then a vice-president at NBC Sports and later became the head of ESPN. He asked me to work the NCAA regional play-offs in Tuscaloosa, Alabama. I had been hoping the NBC people would call.

I had no idea whom I was working with down there. I just went to the game. I didn't know any NBC people. When I got to the hotel, the desk clerk said, "Oh, yeah, Mr. Gowdy has checked in, too."

Just like a typical fan, I thought, "Curt Gowdy! Are you kidding me? I'm going to work with Curt Gowdy!" He was NBC Sports's top broadcaster. I wondered why I was doing the game with him. I had assumed that I'd be working as just one of the guys, and Gowdy would be doing the big game wherever that was. I met him that night. He was very cordial. Curt was very interested in western art and invited me to go view some paintings with him the next morning. He seemed very sophisticated for a sports announcer.

The game, as I explained earlier, was the matchup between Al McGuire's Marquette team and Kentucky. When
the weekend was over, and Kentucky had won, I felt a tinge
of the big time. I admit it. I remember thinking about the
thrill of telling my grandkids about it. Anyhow, both the
game and the dream ended, and I left Tuscaloosa and went
home. I was real happy. I'd done a game with Curt Gowdy,
the elite of broadcasting. But then that ol' nervous pang hit
me, and I thought, "I wonder if they'll want me to do another
game."

I got home and spent several days hoping the NBC people
would call me to do next week's game. But the more I waited,
the more I began to think that was unrealistic. They had
probably already made a move on the next games. After all,
these were the regionals. Finally, on Wednesday I got a call
from Scotty Connal. He said, "Billy, you really did a nice job
for us. We want to include you in our assignments for this
week."

I jumped at it. "Well, fine. I'm available to do whatever you
need me to."

He said, "We want you to go to Portland."

"Who will I be working with?" I asked.

"Oh," he said, "you'll be working with Curt again. He likes
the way you work with him."

I went to Portland without even thinking about who was
playing. I was just excited to be working with Curt again.
Then it hit me. Hell, UCLA was there. Now, UCLA was a
good club but not a team to win it all. John Wooden had Dave
Meyers, Marques Johnson, Richard Washington, Ralph Drol-
linger, Andre McCarter, and Pete Trgovich. Nobody knew it
at the time, but this was Wooden's last team. It was really
made up of overachievers.

An interesting thing happened that weekend. The team
favored to win that region was Arizona State. They had great
quickness and a terrific pressing team. In the first round,
UCLA played Montana, coached by Jud Heathcoate, and won
the game, 67-64. The referee had inadvertently knocked out
the star player on Heathcoate's team, which had been leading

at the time. The ref had turned to give the guy the ball on an out-of-bounds play and hit him in the head and knocked him out. UCLA then came back and won.

The win sent the Bruins against Arizona State, Ned Walk's team. I remember going to Arizona State's practice and watching them review everything UCLA did. They went over every play and every move. The players stood and listened for what seemed like hours on end. Then UCLA came out and practiced. John Wooden had the very important ability to identify and focus on what things were going to be critical. He didn't really worry about the opponent as much as he did his own players' execution and style. His team went through normal exercises, shooting drills, passing drills, very basic things. Then Wooden set up how they would bring the ball inbounds against the Arizona State press. It seemed he went through the whole session without ever mentioning Arizona State. I'll never forget one thing. Wooden was setting up his players in position, and he told Marques Johnson to stand in a certain place. Wooden then got ready to put the ball inbounds, but stopped and very calmly said, "No, Marques, not there. Here." He moved Johnson about six inches and then they executed the play. He was remarkable in focusing his players' concentration. He enabled them to execute the finer points of the game. The six inches probably didn't have that much to do with the success of the play, but it had everything to do with concentration.

Marques Johnson had a big day, scoring 30-some points, and the Bruins moved on to the Final Four. It was fun, but I figured I had run my string for that year. There was only one thing left to do in college basketball that year, the national championship. Doing a Final Four had been a goal of mine, but I assumed that NBC had made plans for somebody else to broadcast it. Then, on Tuesday, I got a call from NBC. The network people wanted me in San Diego to do the game. I was sky-high.

I had spent what amounted to three weeks with Curt Gowdy and the other top-notch NBC people, including Roy Hammerman, their lead producer. In that time, I had begun to perceive a great deal of insecurity among those people. They had reached the top of the profession, but the heights only seemed to make them worry about someone taking their places someday. I could really sense that in San Diego, even among the technical crew. In those days, the networks didn't do basketball during the regular season. So this three-week run of games was just another assignment for them. For me, it was basketball heaven. For those guys, it was just another week of doing basketball as opposed to football or hockey or something else—just another day at the office. That became more apparent to me over the course of the tournament. I couldn't understand how it could ever get to be that way. I decided then that, if I ever got in that rut, that would be the moment I would walk away from broadcasting, no matter where it was.

In those days Curt Gowdy was at the top of the charts as a broadcaster. He was doing the Rose Bowl, the World Series, the NCAA basketball championship. He was doing more big events than all other announcers put together. There didn't seem to be any reason for Curt to be concerned about the future. But he had had some problems with his neck, and he seemed a little low. That was never noticeable on the air, but off camera it was obvious he wasn't doing well. Curt invited me to ride along with him to the championship game between Kentucky and UCLA. A guy named Al Davis was going to ride with us. I soon realized he was the same Al Davis who owned the Oakland (now the Los Angeles) Raiders. Curt, of course, had done as much as anybody from a public relations standpoint to help dignify the American Football League, when he and Jack Christiansen broadcast the games. Over the years, Curt and Al Davis had become close friends.

When we got into the limo, Curt was in the front seat and Al and I sat in the back. I'll never forget what happened.

Al complimented me on my broadcasting. And Curt showed some irritation.

"Al, that's the problem," he said. "They're all taking about the young guys, the up-and-coming guys. Nobody's talking about me anymore."

I was shocked at that because I idolized Curt Gowdy. I was sure everybody else did too. But it struck me that he was sensing that he was about to lose his position, that he couldn't stay at the top of broadcasting forever. It really upset me that he was worried about that because he had accomplished so much as a broadcaster. I wanted to tell him, "Who cares what anybody thinks? Hey, you've done more big games and done more for sports than anybody could ever do again. You'll go down in broadcast history as one of the greatest."

The ride really depressed me.

The semifinal game was a great matchup between Wooden and his former student and player, Denny Crum, the University of Louisville coach. Crum had the superior team and was primed to win. Today, if those coaches were to meet with the same teams, Louisville would win handily. I think that Denny Crum has matured that much as a coach, and how could Wooden get any better? He was at the peak of his profession. UCLA had that trapping press, and Wooden used his guards to control the game's tempo. He would speed the game up and then slow it down. Despite all of that, Louisville had the game won. They went to the foul line with Terry Howard, who hadn't missed a free throw all year, something like 31 for 31. Well, he missed the shot, and UCLA put the press on Louisville, stole the ball, and won the game. It was phenomenal. I sat there saying, "There's no way this UCLA team, despite the heritage and everything, even belongs here. They should have been beaten by Montana."

The game ended, UCLA winning 75–74 in overtime. Denny Crum gave the impression of being a hotshot. He had been Wooden's assistant, and although they had developed a heated rivalry, most people thought Crum would someday go back to coach at UCLA. But that day, he had just gotten caught by the master. I felt sorry for the kid for missing the foul shot, but everyone sensed that it was in the cards that UCLA was going to advance.

I'll never forget the postgame news conference. I like to go to conferences when time permits because the reporters sometimes throw good questions at the coaches. You get to see a side of a coach or a player you might not have otherwise seen. And the press conferences give me a chance to compare notes, to see if what I said during the broadcast was on target with how the coaches viewed the game.

I walked into this press conference, and Wooden was already there. A reporter asked him something about the game, and Wooden responded in so many words that he had enjoyed coaching this last team as much as he had his first team. It was like the ceiling had fallen in. People looked at each other and asked, "Did he say this was his last team?"

Suddenly, everybody reacted. The hands started going crazy, waving in the air to ask a question like kids in a classroom. "Do you mean Monday night will be it?" they asked. "Did you just announce your retirement?"

Basically, he had done just that. Wooden ended his career just as he had coached during it: with subtlety. No big press conferences. No UCLA announcement that John Wooden was retiring. That was it. No big deal. Boy, the reporters scurried to the phones. Everybody was going crazy trying to call the story in. Suddenly, the big question in San Diego became the identity of Wooden's successor. It just so happened that the next guy to be interviewed after Wooden was Denny Crum, the guy everybody assumed would be the next UCLA coach. It was a hot seat for Denny. Reporters began firing questions about whether he would replace Wooden. Unfortunately for UCLA, it didn't work out that way. Had Crum been the man selected, the school probably would have retained its rank in the basketball world.

That Monday night was my first national championship game, but it was almost anticlimactic after Wooden's announcement. UCLA brushed past Kentucky in the final to give "the Wizard of Westwood" a retirement gift.

Curt Gowdy remained uneasy throughout the tournament. He seemed to sense something coming, although he was a very valuable and powerful talent at NBC. Today, talent seldom becomes that powerful, at least not in the two networks I've been involved with. Decisions are made, and the talent is brought in only for consultation, seldom as part of the decision-making process. But somehow, Curt knew that NBC was getting ready for some new blood.

Despite the pallor cast by Curt's situation, the end of the season left me with a pretty good feeling. I had almost two years of network experience under my belt. I had received good reviews from the TV critics, and the network people seemed pleased with my work. But, looking back on it, I was in an uneasy position. I had worked my way into the National Championship broadcast. But I wasn't affiliated with a network station, like KNBC or NBC-NY. There was no inside power, where a station executive might be able to pull some strings and help me out. And I wasn't a guy of national reputation, not a player who had just set new records in the NBA and was now shifting into broadcasting. I hadn't been a college head coach. I was just a fan, an advertising salesman, a former ACC player and assistant coach. But basically, just a fan. All of a sudden, I was an unknown guy on the scene, doing the National Championship game. I was nothing but part-time help, getting paid $750 a game, game by game. On the other hand, that was also my best asset. I wasn't involved in the power struggle. I had no ambition to be a Madison Avenue guy who held up the networks with money demands, negotiations, and agents.

I went home to Winston-Salem, honored that I had been given a chance to do the big game. And I was eager to do the ACC telecast again if and when Chesley ever called me. A funny thing about Ches, though. Here I had graduated to doing the National Championship game, but I never got a letter from him saying I did a good job or anything. As usual, I didn't hear from him until a week before the ACC started the next year. But I felt secure in the off-season. I'd worked four games for NBC and made $3,000. Hell, I would've given my right arm to do those games. Just to be there.

Eddie Einhorn's dream came true with the 1975–76 college basketball season. NBC bought his idea of broadcasting regular-season college basketball games. No network had ever done it before. In fulfilling his dream, Einhorn helped dozens of other people, including Dick Enberg and me, realize theirs.

C. D. Chesley's idea had been to make a profit on each and every ACC game, each and every year. He wanted to do a quality job with a limited product. Einhorn's goal was to make college basketball the big hit. He wanted to put together all of college basketball in a package, hold the rights to it, and then sell it off to a network. Both men fulfilled their dreams. Eddie made his big hit, and Ches always made a profit. Today, Eddie Einhorn holds interests in a variety of enterprises, including part ownership of the Chicago White Sox and franchises of indoor soccer and the USFL. But he should always be known as one of the major figures in the rise of college basketball.

There were good reasons for NBC to get involved in the regular season. This thing called the NCAA tournament seemed to be picking up momentum, and the college basketball game on Super Bowl Sunday was a nice prelude to the football battle. The basketball game got great ratings. The time was right. Eddie had the whole thing put together and did a hell of a selling job on NBC. Working as a consultant, Eddie Einhorn became a coordinator of the network's coverage.

In building his dream, Eddie Einhorn had been responsible for developing a guy who was to become one of the hottest properties in all of broadcasting, Dick Enberg. Dick was doing games for TVS, Eddie's production company, on the West Coast for the Pac 10 (the Pac 8 in those days). That assignment included the UCLA games at the apex of John Wooden's heyday. Einhorn considered Enberg the best play-by-play broadcaster in the country, even though Dick didn't have a national reputation then. Chesley considered me the best color man. NBC officials really didn't have an opinion, except that they'd used me the previous year, and they were listening to Eddie's recommendations on Enberg. They liked Enberg. He was the kind of guy they wanted to hire for the total picture, all their sports. But the NBC people needed a niche to bring him on board, and that niche was college basketball.

Enberg and I had worked together once before, a 1975 Super Bowl Sunday game between Maryland and UCLA. That broadcast was also the first joint production by the two rivals in televised college basketball, Chesley and Einhorn. They had a reason to merge, a need, at least for that one game. Chesley had the rights to the ACC, and he had Maryland, which was a top team. And Einhorn had the Pac 8 and UCLA, which made a great match up for Super Bowl Sunday. They had a major East Coast city, Washington, a major West Coast city, Los Angeles. One of Chesley's strengths was production ability. Einhorn probably wouldn't have admitted it, but Chesley's production was superior. On the other hand, Einhorn had the capability of putting together a broadcast for syndication to an independent network of stations nationwide. He did games in most of the other conferences, and he worked with a lot of stations. He could go to those stations and pull them into a national game. It was a good marriage.

There were, however, a few problems. One was the name of the broadcast. Was it going to be TVS-Chesley or Chesley-TVS? Who comes on the air first? Chesley's announcers or Einhorn's? Both sides thought the announcers would give the viewers an impression of which company was doing the game. There was even a question about what patches would be worn on the broadcast team's jackets. Thank goodness I wasn't a party to all that nonsense.

I was simply told to go to the game with my broadcasting partner, Jim Thacker. We assumed we would work the game together. We didn't know Einhorn had told Enberg to work the game. So Dick Enberg, who had a very busy broadcasting schedule on the West Coast, flew across country to announce the game. It was as big a thing for him as it was for us. Enberg's previous big assignment, other than California Angels baseball and Pac 8 basketball, had been the 1968 UCLA/Houston game featuring Elvin Hayes and Lew Alcindor (now Kareem Abdul-Jabbar). That was the first nationally televised college basketball game. Einhorn had put it together, and Enberg had broadcast it.

The morning of the game, Chesley told me at breakfast that there was a little problem. Einhorn had insisted that Enberg be the announcer. Chesley said he was going to give in, and they had worked out an agreement. I would be the color man, and Enberg and Thacker would each handle the play-by-play for a half. While one did the broadcast, the other would work the floor, looking for feature extras. Chesley and Einhorn agreed that Enberg would open the game and do the first half.

I knew Thacker like the back of my hand. He's really a quality person, and I knew he would be understanding and do everything possible to make the broadcast professional. Not that Thacker could do anything about the screwy situation, but he was high-caliber and would make it work.

I didn't know Enberg. But I figured him for some LA hotshot. He gave me the impression that he thought that everything about him was just perfect. I didn't get to have dinner with him when I first met him, so I couldn't sense too much about him. But if anything, he seemed a little snobbish. I couldn't wait for the production meeting, where they were going to inform these guys that they weren't going to work the whole game. That's where I would learn more.

I focused my eyes right on Enberg, so that when they announced how the broadcast was going to be handled, I could see how he reacted. It would tell me an awful lot about him as a person. I'll never forget how Dick reacted. Of course, now that I've known him for a long time and admire him as a person and a friend, it doesn't surprise me at all. But back then, I thought the guy would go into a temper tantrum or something. I expected something like, "What do you mean I'm not going to do the whole game?" But, boy, he took it right. His eyes never blinked. He was positive and upbeat, asking what he could help do while he was down on the floor. He may have been really pissed off inside, but nobody would ever have known it. I thought he had a lot of class.

I announced the game with him, and he had his whole act

together. He was a super pro and fun to work with. So that brief marriage between Chesley and Einhorn also set up the forerunner of the NBC college basketball broadcast team. When the NBC executives bought Einhorn's college basketball package, Enberg was the guy they wanted for the play-by-play. Basketball became the means by which the network could work him into other assignments. Eventually, he became their premier broadcaster.

As for me, Scotty Connal wanted me to do the color, but the network people needed to make sure they got someone Enberg would be comfortable working with. As Dick recalls the story, he told the NBC people that he really didn't need anybody to do the color in a college basketball game. He felt he was very capable of doing the game by himself with one exception. If NBC could guarantee that every game would be a good one, there would be no problems working alone. But if the network couldn't guarantee that, then Enberg wanted somebody to work with him during the moments when the game didn't carry itself. He told them that, if they were going to hire somebody, he would like to work with me. That fit in nicely with NBC's plans. They didn't have to go out and find someone else.

So that's how Enberg and Packer got started. I hadn't considered that my work at NBC might conflict with the ACC games I had been doing. I hadn't considered that schedules would be a problem. I told NBC, "Oh, sure, I'd love to do it." I figured I'd do a national game once a week with Dick Enberg, and it would be the greatest thing since sliced bread. But I forgot all about Chesley and the ACC. I figured I'd do the ACC when I could. The only problem was that most of those games wound up being on the same days as my network assignments.

When Ches heard about it, he came to see me and said, "Billy, you don't have the ambition to be a broadcaster. You don't want to get into that rat race. Just do my games and forget those people." For the first time in my life, money became a factor in my decision. Chesley was paying $175 a game, and NBC was talking about paying me $1,800. I thought, "Wait a minute. Twenty games at $1,800 a game. That's $36,000 a year. I'm doing 20 games at $175 a game."

So I said, "Wait a minute, Mr. Chesley. You've been great to me, but I've also done a pretty good job for you. I think I better go home and consider my family a little bit here."

That was the first time it really hit me that this was becoming a profession, not just a lark, a little side money for the family and a great bunch of fun for me. I had to tell Ches I was going to work for NBC. Looking back on it, it's comical to think that the decision would even be a matter of discussion. I mean here was a network offering me $36,000 to Chesley's $3,500. But Chesley and I discussed it seriously on a number of occasions, and I finally had to tell him no. It was almost telling your father that you're going to do something he doesn't want you to do.

As strange as it might seem, the situation served to bring Chesley and me quite a bit closer. After I'd worked a few national games, I went to him and said, "You know, Ches, I'd still like to work the ACC games if you want me to, when they're not in conflict with the national games." He said he'd like to have me, and I thought it would be a great deal of fun. And it would keep me on my toes. When you work a league as tough as the Atlantic Coast Conference, you're on trial each and every ball game. It's like a referee with a good reputation. He can't rest on his laurels. Each game is a challenge to his abilities, regardless of how well he worked the night before. Past games mean little to the fans. They're interested in the one you're working, waiting to see if you let a little bias slip through.

The ACC is rabid for basketball. Everyone—the guy on the corner, the grocery store man, the gas station attendant—follows the teams and has strong loyalties. And they really keep you on your toes. To tell the truth, the money for the national games was great, but I missed working in the heart of the regional enthusiasm.

Money was the only hitch to resuming work with Chesley. There was quite a difference between what the network paid and what he had to offer. Rather than his usual informality, this time Ches wanted to make sure that I understood he couldn't pay me what the network did. We discussed it for a while, and I said, "You know, Ches, I really would do the games for you for nothing. But what I'd like to do is have an opportunity to sell some advertising time. And if you'll give me that opportunity with a percentage of the sales, I can afford to do the ball games as a hobby, which is the way I'd like to consider doing them anyway."

We settled on an agreement, and I promptly went out and in about 35 days acquired a number of sponsors for Atlantic Coast Conference basketball. What was so funny is that Ches didn't even give me a rate card to show what the spots were selling for. Even in those days, we were talking about pretty sizable packages for companies to sponsor the games, in excess of $100,000 each. So I called him up and said, "Ches, I've got four people very interested in being involved in ACC basketball next year. How about giving me a price range so I can tell them what they're going to have to pay?"

Ches didn't believe me. As a matter of fact, he was very hesitant about giving me a rate card. I don't even know if he had one in those days. He still kind of played things by the seat of his pants. He knew what he wanted to have on the bottom line and always worked things out to make it. I finally convinced him that I had to have a price if I was going to close these sales. Since he didn't believe I really had the customers in line, he gave me the prices.

I secured the advertisers. They agreed on the price, and I called Ches back and told him I would need contracts to sign the new business. He seemed caught at a loss for words. He realized I really did have people in line. When I told him who the clients were, and that one was a car company, he said, "I'm sorry, you can't use that automotive client because I'm going to sell to Toyota again this year."

I said, "Gee, Ches, I wish you had told me that in advance." Then I told him about the next client, the McDonald's franchise in North and South Carolina. He said, "We can't use McDonald's because I'm going to get Hardee's to renew."

Finally I told him, "Ches, you don't have an airline, and I

have Piedmont ready to commit." He said, "I can't believe
Piedmont would want to come in." He finally realized I was
very capable of selling advertising in his marketplace. We
had a few squabbles over commissions, but the agreement
soon proved enlightening and lucrative for me. To this day, I
thank Chesley—he's dead now—for getting me involved in
television. Frankly, the business side of it has been every bit
as interesting as the broadcasting.

The best part of it all was that I was able to resume
broadcasting ACC games when schedules didn't conflict with
network assignments. Deep in my heart, I was still pretty
much a Chesley man and an ACC fan, a fact that didn't
escape some viewers. At first, I caught some heat from people
around the country over that. But, hell, I love basketball. If I
lived in Houston, I'd be a Southwest Conference man; in
Chicago, I'd follow Loyola. I kept doing those ACC games
because I loved it. Still, it caused me to be perceived as biased
toward the ACC, which I wasn't.

Bobby Knight had jabbed home the problem that year—as
only Bobby can do—just before the 1976 semifinals game in
the Spectrum in Philadelphia. He had brought his undefeated team on the floor to face UCLA. It was undoubtedly a
coup for the Big 10, with two teams—Indiana and Michigan—in the Final Four. Both teams would make it to the
finals Monday night, while the ACC tournament entries—
North Carolina and Virginia—had lost in the first round of
regional tournament play. I was over at the scorer's table,
waiting for the game to begin. Knight was at his bench,
kneeling with his players. I looked up, and he motioned me
over. I thought it must be something really important, so I
hustled over. As I walked up, Knight looked up from his
players and said with a snicker, "Packer, where the shit is the
ACC now?"

Then he quickly looked away and didn't say anything else,
didn't even look back at me. I was left standing there,
humiliated, feeling like a fool. There was no opportunity to
respond, nothing I could say. He didn't give me a chance.

After a few moments of standing there, stunned, I turned and walked back.

Bobby Knight had had himself a little fun at my expense. It wasn't the first time, and it wouldn't be the last. We've developed a good relationship over the years, one based on give and take.

A lot of people have a hard time understanding Bobby. But really his sense of humor is no different than the other facets of his personality. Everything he does is very incisive. Lately, Bobby's critics have taken to interpreting his incisiveness and demand for excellence as even greater proof that he's a humongous jerk. That's wrong. A lot of people don't understand his values.

Above all, Bobby Knight is dedicated to doing everything he does to the best of his ability. A lot of people say that about themselves. Bobby Knight is one of the few people who really mean it. And he demands that dedication from the people around him. At times, those strong convictions tend to blind him to other people's feelings. Sometimes he holds his convictions to a fault, and obviously that's caused him some problems.

But the people who criticize him often are responding to the superficial circumstances of a controversy. For example, Bobby may become angry with a referee. But what has really ticked him off is that he thinks the official isn't hustling and working hard on the floor, which has led to bad calls. This may sound odd, but I have a lot of respect for Bobby as a human being. He's much deeper than people think.

If anything, my business and broadcasting experience with Chesley made me more valuable to the network. Dick Enberg and I quickly found success doing the NBC games. The newspaper critics were good to us. The network people liked it. The college people accepted us as a solid broadcast team, and we were on our way as a twosome. It worked out very well until that 1976 National Championship in Philadelphia. Several days before it began, I got a screwy kind of phone call

from Chet Simmons (who became commissioner of the
United States Football League), the president of NBC
Sports. He said he wanted to talk to me about what could
become a serious problem in Philadelphia.

"Sure," I said and thought, "I'm going to talk to Chet
Simmons face to face. I wonder what's up. Maybe *I'm* the
problem."

It turned out that Curt Gowdy had a clause in his contract
allowing him to announce the National Championship. And
Dick Enberg's agent was taking the position that, if he was
pulled off that game, in effect, it would look like he wasn't
good enough to do the National Championship game. That
would be a slap in the face and hurt his career. Both sides had
a legitimate situation there. NBC was caught between a rock
and a hard place. For the Saturday semifinals, they decided
I would announce one game with Dick and the other with
Curt. Curt would come on the air first, so the viewers
wouldn't know who was the host and who was the play-by-
play man. That would make it look as if Curt and Dick shared
top billing.

"Now, this could be a real problem," the network people
said, "because these two guys may not like each other. One
may grab the mike from the other, and, Billy, you'll be in the
middle. We want you to handle it gracefully."

I thought to myself, "You've got to be kidding. I know both
of these guys. These are two of the sharpest people you'd ever
want to meet. They are both super professionals, and there's
no way they're going to go on the air and ever give any hint
of personal rivalry to the fans." I was absolutely positive that
they wouldn't.

Things were handled according to plan. Dick worked one
of the games, Curt worked the other, and then they took turns
being host to lead into the games. It worked fine, and of
course, both guys were very cordial to one another. Still,
there was an air of competition about the broadcast. With
Gowdy, you're talking about the guy who has been the king of
NBC sports broadcasting, and in Enberg, you had the guy
who was taking his place. Curt had sensed a changing of the

guard. Dick wasn't out to attack Curt or anything. It was just that the time had come.

The Monday night championship required more adjustments. The network brass decided that Curt and Dick would share the game, and I would be the odd man out. But they didn't want me to be too far out because Curt and Dick weren't really into the technical aspects of the game. The network people sent me to New York to work in the studio with two guys I'd never heard of, Len Leonard and Bryant Gumbel, who was just breaking in as an NBC sports anchor. My job was to do the blackboard routine: come on before the game and explain some technical things and then again at the half and after the game to chart what had happened. I was willing to do whatever was necessary for the broadcast, although I hated not being able to see the game live. But I figured everyone at NBC studios in New York would be excited. To me, there wasn't a bigger thing happening in the world than the National Championship.

When I arrived at the studio, the guy at the front desk asked me what I wanted.

"Well, I'm here for the National Championship," I said.

Oh, yeah, he said, that's in studio such and such.

I went there and found Len Leonard and Bryant Gumbel. We talked, and Leonard didn't waste any time before he started belittling basketball. He began making fun of the championship, saying things like "What's this baskets stuff? What the hell is basketball?" I got kind of miffed and took the attitude "What do you mean? This championship is the biggest thing on the face of the earth right now." To Leonard it was a joke.

But this guy Bryant Gumbel was really into it. He asked some in-depth questions, and I could tell he was a sports fan. He was enthused about what could happen in the game. We traded opinions. He knew a lot about basketball. Then the other studio people started talking about a pool. I thought they were starting up a little in-house gambling on the game. All the technicians and editorial aides were jumping in. But it was for the Academy Awards—who was going to be the best actor, best supporting actor, that kind of thing—not basketball. I was so far removed from that world I didn't even know who had been nominated. Hell, I didn't even know the Academy Awards were on. I said to myself, "What we're talking about tonight is college basketball. National Championship. What are the Academy Awards?" They had to be kidding. Furthermore, I was annoyed as a businessman and broadcaster. First, the crew members didn't have their minds 100 percent on what they were supposed to be doing. Second, basketball was on the network that was paying their salaries. They shouldn't even have worried about what was on another network. Not only were they concerned about it and interested in it; they were watching it.

Bryant and I basically watched the basketball game alone. I was charting and keeping stats and telling the technicians which sequences to keep for replays. The studio people were openly annoyed, taking the attitude that "This son of a bitch Packer is a crazy man; nobody cares about that basketball game." I could feel the tension building. I was really in the way of their enjoyable evening watching the Academy Awards. But, as I said, one night out of the year, the NCAA basketball championship is the most important event on earth. And that night nothing could top it. Not even the Academy Awards.

At that point in my career, I was still getting paid by the game, and I started thinking I'd be smart to have a guaranteed contract. I didn't know if some network executive might decide he didn't like what I was doing and try to knock me out of the booth. I saw what was happening to Curt, and I thought I'd better have some protection. Scotty Connal arranged a meeting for me in New York with Bob Dunne, a negotiator for NBC. I went in figuring that things would be great if I could make $35,000 or $36,000 a year. So I walked in there without an agent, without any real idea of what I should be paid. But $36,000 seemed like a damn nice number to me. If I didn't do anything else in the course of the year, I could feed my family on that.

Mr. Dunne, who's a very nice guy, greeted me with "Billy, it's just great to see you. You've done a hell of a job for us. We're really proud of what you've done. What can we do for you?"

That made me feel good. I said, "Well, Mr. Dunne, I'd like to get on a regular basis here. I'd like to know what I'll be paid next year. And I'd like to be the college basketball analyst of NBC. I'll do whatever assignments you send me for a flat fee."

He said, "Fine. How much do you think we ought to pay you?"

And I said, "$36,000."

He said, "$36,000? That sounds fair to me. Anything else you need?"

I thought, "Packer, you dumb jerk. Evidently, you're worth more than that. He didn't even bat an eyelash." I felt like a fool. I'd heard Dick Enberg talk about per diem money, so I asked him about a per diem.

He said, "Well, what do you think? Will $50 cover it?" I thought I'd been low on the other number, so I figured I'd better raise him on this one. The whole conversation didn't last 10 minutes. I said, "Well, gee, I go to some big cities, and I don't think $50 will handle it."

So he said, "How about $75 then?" I said, "Okay, $75." I thought the per diem covered everything—cabs, hotel rooms and food, all that stuff. I figured I'd kill them with $75 for expenses. But then Dunne added, "And, of course, we'll pick up all the hotel and ground transportation."

Suddenly, I realized I had $75 a day to blow on food and newspapers. I'd be making another $50 a day on the game. "I've really made a hit here," I thought.

Then he said, "Billy, before you leave, I'd like to take you down and introduce you to some of our executives here at NBC. I know that they'd be happy to know that you're on board with us now on a permanent basis."

I was thinking how happy I was to get the contract down. I wanted to call my wife and tell her I just made a big hit here in New York. Although I was eager to get out of the place and celebrate, we walked down the hall, where he took me in to meet this executive. This guy had an office about 30 by 30, and he was standing over against the wall. As I walked in, I thought, "This guy doesn't want to see me. He won't know who the hell I am, and I'm embarrassed that I'm going to see somebody who won't know me from Adam." So I tried to think of something important to say to the guy so he would think I'm sharp. I recalled that the network's technicians were on strike and that the NBC executives were having to work as technicians to replace them. In my cab on the way from the airport, I read in the *New York Daily News* that the strike had just ended that day. I figured I'd be smart and comment on that.

As Dunne introduced me, I could tell the guy had no idea who I was or what I did. I didn't want to embarrass him any more than I was embarrassed already. So when he said it was great to have me on board and all the customary bull, I said, "Gee, I guess all you guys up here are really happy that the strike's over."

He looked at me, stunned, and asked, "It's over?!"

Here it was 10:30 in the morning, and I had read it on the front page of the *Daily News.* Once again I'd run into the New York City network syndrome. I'd just assumed that the guys in those high positions are really in touch with what's going on. They aren't. I got out of there and whistled all the way back to Winston-Salem.

CHAPTER

6

THE McGUIRE ANGLE

Our Packer-Enberg twosome became a threesome in 1978 with the arrival of Al McGuire. Al knew the transition from coach to broadcaster would be difficult, and at times, it was. Overnight, Al had become a broadcasting tenderfoot. And Dick and I didn't miss the opportunity to have a little fun at his expense.

We did a game at the University of Texas, probably the only time the basketball Longhorns have ever appeared on network television. Abe Lemons had done a heck of a job building the program and had won the NIT in 1977. He had a very strong team coming back that next year, and we at NBC decided to match his squad against Southern Cal, where Bob Boyd was developing a fine team. The game was billed as quite an attraction, and we were set to give it even more buildup in our pregame show.

We had a standard procedure for pregame shows in which Al and I would take turns previewing opposing teams. Dick would open the show and then throw it to Al. Al would always go first because, in his first year of broadcasting, he didn't like to wear the earpiece announcers wear. With the earpiece, announcers can hear instructions from the broadcast truck, an important aid because broadcasters base their timing on the countdowns from the truck. However, Al didn't like it because when someone started talking to him through his earpiece he would have to stop talking and listen. It was annoying for him. So we always let Al go first to prevent timing problems.

Al would talk about his team, emphasizing the prominent player. And then Dick would throw it to me, and I would do the same about the opposing team. With both of us listening to our earpieces, Dick and I would know how much time we had left to finish the segment. I would then throw it back to Dick before cutting to a commercial.

Al had very quickly gotten into the habit of using cue cards with players' names for his half of the opening. Dick and I assumed he had them there only as a security blanket, not as a matter of necessity. To prove a point, we decided to pull a little trick on Al. We told the broadcast assistant holding the cue cards to drop them just as Dick threw it to Al that day.

Al's assignment was to talk about Southern Cal's outstanding young forward, Cliff Robinson. Al had his cue cards set up with all those cute phrases he uses, like "He's a rocket buster. He pierces the clouds. He scrapes dust off the backboards"—the usual McGuire stuff in those days. Well, just as Dick threw it to Al, the assistant did just as we told him and dropped the cards. Unfortunately, Al had no idea who Cliff Robinson was. But without blinking, Al launched into his lines: "Well, Dick," he said, "you know Ole Treetop. He's a heck of a ball player." He went on talking about "Ole Treetop" for a while. I sat there in disbelief. I didn't even know Robinson had the nickname Treetop.

When we finally broke to a commercial, I asked Al how he knew the guy's nickname.

"I had no idea whether his name was Treetop [which it wasn't]," he said, "but without those cue cards I didn't know anything, period. So I just started calling him Treetop and hoped I could get through the deal."

We had a lot of laughs during the season. While Al didn't know the names and faces, we worked things out as a threesome and eventually came up with a pretty good product. It all worked fine until the NCAA tournament, when the circumstances quickly turned somber.

The problem began when NBC executives decided not to look at us as a threesome. They figured they had a depth of talent. They viewed Enberg as a play-by-play guy and McGuire and me as analysts, both able to handle the analysis job alone. The executives decided there was no reason to keep us together during the NCAA tournament. They put Dick and me together and paired Al with Curt Gowdy. And for the championship game, they reasoned they could bring Enberg, Packer, and McGuire back together while keeping Gowdy as a host. That was the game plan.

But the executives really didn't understand that Al McGuire couldn't be an analyst. At least not by himself. Al didn't know any players; he didn't know any coaches. He really didn't know a lot about technical basketball, not to interpret it. He knew all about basketball for his own purposes, but he didn't know how to relay that to the network audience. When Al first started broadcasting college basketball, he couldn't name or identify by picture 10 coaches or 5 players in the entire country. If you asked him whom he favored to win the WAC, he wouldn't have known, wouldn't even have cared who those people were. That was all immaterial to him. And if the network brass had asked Al, he would have told them right up front. But nobody asked him. They just assumed, "Hey, the guy coached the national champions. He's got to know all of this stuff." Then again, just about anybody would assume he at least knew the names and faces. Unless they knew Al.

So the executives put Al and Curt together and Dick and me together. Well, all hell broke loose. Curt had not done a college basketball game all year. A broadcaster has to be doing basketball regularly to get into the swing of it and know what's going on. Al had been doing games with us. We had the information. He maybe knew three players. "Give me the names of three players," he would say. "Which ones are they? If they get out of the game, I'll talk about something else. You guys know all that stuff."

In 1978, an analyst had to be pretty well prepared, especially for an NCAA double-header. There were four teams to learn about, plus 20 minutes of time to fill between the games. And chances were that two teams would be unknowns, with unknown players and coaches never seen on the networks before. In those days, the networks didn't throw it back to the New York studios for anchors like Len Berman and Brent Musburger to handle. The analyst and broadcaster had to fill the gaps, leaving no time to regroup and gather their thoughts between games.

Al and Curt's broadcasts were supervised by Michael Weissman, a young, up-and-coming NBC sports producer. He assumed these two professional broadcasters knew what was going on. Somehow, Curt, Al, and Mike got through the first game. Barely. The second half of the double-header pitted UCLA against Kansas. Instead of spending 20 minutes getting ready for the second game, they spent 20 minutes in a broadcast room providing fill time on the air. They got to the court just in time to begin announcing the game and immediately ran into terrible problems. They consistently misidentified a number of players on the floor. The Pac-10 and Big Eight fans following on TV got irate and started buzzing the phone lines at NBC. Nobody in the broadcast truck knew that they weren't pronouncing the names right. To cap it all, Al and Curt got into an argument at the end of the game over who should be the MVP. Al didn't really think it was important anyway and probably wasn't even keeping up with the game. Dick and I usually handled that when we worked with Al, unless he had something funny and off the wall to say.

Al had never had the training or the experience to give Curt support. Curt didn't have the time and hadn't been working on college basketball enough to be prepared. And the producer didn't have the experience to pull them together. So it became a disaster. The press seemed to be waiting for Curt Gowdy to fail. Suddenly, the critics had a chance to get him. They attacked from all areas, and Curt had no excuse that he could offer publicly. He took the brunt of the whole problem. It became national news, with wire-service stories on how Curt Gowdy had screwed up. "NBC to pull Gowdy," the headlines read. It was very, very unfortunate. Al, because of who he was, because he was fresh and likable, didn't get any abuse. Curt got it all.

NBC realized it had a real problem. The executives quickly put Enberg and McGuire back together and paired Curt with me. But the noise didn't stop. The press continued to bombard him. There were even signs in the gymnasiums. Things were said that were totally uncalled for, considering what Curt had done for sports television during his long career. What was worse, the network offered little support because it was time for him to go anyway. Curt went through an unbelievably hard time. It wasn't good for any of us.

The next season went more smoothly, as Al and I got to know each other better. That didn't stop him from punctuating every occasion with his wackiness.

I had worked the first Great Alaskan Shootout in 1978 and was invited back by the tournament promoters, including Rick Ray, in 1979. Ray was just getting his company, Raycom, off the ground and has since moved to the fore as a television syndicator. Ray had invited me back for the second year and asked me to bring Al along. Al and I had begun to develop a friendship. I knew he liked to travel, so it seemed like a good idea. After my first trip, I was convinced that the Shootout could be a good business opportunity. Al and I had discussed it. We were interested in getting involved in a business project together where we could have some fun, make a little money, and build into something bigger and better. The promoters not only wanted us to work the games, but they wanted us to speak at a banquet as well. They asked me if I would be the MC and get Al McGuire to be the key speaker. They agreed to pay him $2,000 for speaking, which seemed to satisfy Al. But then again, I still didn't know him all that well.

Al and I met in Chicago and flew to Alaska. The flight out was one great childish time. First of all, because Al whipped out his clergy card, we sneaked into first class where we didn't belong. Al has a card that shows he's clergy. He also has a card for handicapped parking, and he uses these whenever he needs to get some kind of advantage. (Al saves quite a bit of money whenever he goes to the Milwaukee airport because he has clergy stickers all over his car. He drives a 1965 Oldsmobile that he parks right up front, and he never gets charged for anything.)

In the first-class section, we had a contest to see who could collect the most pairs of the airline's complimentary slippers. We sneaked back and forth from our seats, stealing people's slippers as they snoozed. The slippers were blue and red, so we gave ourselves a certain number of points for blue and a certain number for red. I don't remember who won.

Upon our arrival in Anchorage, I was kind of excited, thinking I was embarking on my first business adventure with Al. I got up to leave the plane, but he remained seated.

"Come on, Al," I said. "Let's get going."

He said, "Now wait a minute. You realize Alaska is a long, long way from Milwaukee, Wisconsin."

"I know that," I said.

He looked at me and started again, "I'll probably never come back to Alaska again, but I'm going to have to come back if I don't get paid."

"Al, these are nice people out here," I said. "I'm sure we're going to get paid."

He wasn't swayed. "Well, you don't know we're going to get paid."

"Al, I would imagine these people are trustworthy enough to pay us."

He said, "Well, I'll tell you what I'm going to do. I'm going to stay here in the airplane. You go out and meet the reception committee and tell them to get me my check. When they get me my check, I'll get off the plane."

I kind of laughed. I thought he was just kidding around. Then, after a few moments, I realized that he was serious. So I got off the plane and met the members of the committee. They wanted to know where Al was.

I said, "Oh, he's here. He's on the plane, and he'll be happy to come off and talk to the press here. But he wants to make sure that somebody here has got his check."

As I said that, Al stepped to the doorway of the plane. They could see his head sticking out. He had one foot in Alaska and the other on the plane. I said, "Fellas, he'll come all the way out here if someone will write him his check for his speech. I'll make sure he makes the speech. But he wants to make sure that he gets that check, so he doesn't take off for Milwaukee and doesn't have to come chase somebody for his money."

The committee members all laughed and thought this McGuire was a heck of a nice fella, and wasn't he funny? But Al hadn't designed that little conversation to be funny at all. He was again teaching me a little lesson: that many times after you leave, people forget who you are. They wrote Al his check, and he got off the plane for his first and only Alaska Shootout.

That year, 1979, North Carolina State, coached by Norm Sloan, was one of the teams in the Great Alaskan Shootout. Sloan, of course, has had a tremendous record as a collegiate coach. He's been coach of the year in three different conferences. I don't believe anybody in the history of the collegiate game has ever done that before, and probably no one will ever do it again. On top of that, he led his North Carolina State Wolfpack to the 1974 National Championship. Norman had an excellent team going to the Great Alaskan Shootout that year. He's a very fiery and competitive coach and was primed to begin a successful season.

I didn't have a lot of friends in Alaska and thought I would spend some time with the NC State contingent there. Much to my surprise, when I ran into Sloan at courtside he was ready to take off his jacket and go for a fistfight. He was angry over a talk I had given to the Norfolk Sports Club a week earlier. I was giving a little rundown on the teams in the Atlantic Coast Conference and commented that North Carolina State had some great athletic talent, maybe the best athletes in the conference. But I questioned whether the Wolfpack had an intelligent team. The comment wasn't meant to reflect on the academic background of the players. But the team played physically, using their talent without really exhibiting any leadership quality.

Norman had taken that to mean he was recruiting players who were academically inferior. And that really made him angry. So instead of running into an old friend from Carolina, I locked horns with a coach ready to fight. Norman really challenged me that day. I was shocked by his attitude. I didn't know why he was in a huff, but I was ready to fight, too, if he was going to act like that. It was a good thing for both of us that tempers were calmed by the NC State athletic department officials. A fistfight would have been bad for both of us and a heck of a way to start the college basketball season. As it was, things worked out OK. Al and I had a good time broadcasting. And Norm's team won the second Great Alaska Shootout.

The next incident didn't occur until Al and I were flying back into Chicago. Al was trying to make a flight back to Milwaukee. He seemed to have more trouble getting the 60 miles from Chicago to Milwaukee than I do getting across the country. As we approached O'Hare International, Al pulled another one of his famous moves. This time he convinced the stewardess that he was a member of the clergy, going to Milwaukee for a wedding. He told her he had to take a flight out of another terminal and would need help with a special car to take him across the airport to catch his plane on time. Otherwise, Al told the woman, he might miss the wedding. She was kind enough to radio ahead for Al to make sure a car was waiting when he got off. The stewardess had no idea he was Al McGuire. She assumed he was a minister going to a wedding.

When the plane halted, Al was the first in line to get off. They had an attendant waiting for him right there. But as soon as the door opened, the attendant looked up at him and said, "Al McGuire, what are you doing here?"

Much to the chagrin of the stewardess, she realized she had been had. But arrangements had been made to whisk Al across the airport in a car, so they let him go. He made his flight on time and got back to Milwaukee without much problem. Once again, the streetwise McGuire was way ahead of the game.

Our last regular-season game of that 1979 season was between Notre Dame and Michigan in the Pontiac Silverdome. Because of that, we decided Ann Arbor would make a good setting for our half-hour promo show for the NCAA tournament. We were to do our show at various settings on the University of Michigan campus. Dick Enberg's good friend, Dick Wood, who became a good friend to all of us, lived in Ann Arbor, and Enberg arranged for us to stay at Dick Wood's house the night before shooting. We had a nice dinner at Dick's house, then we were going to retire to the lodge Wood had down by his tennis courts, where Al and I would stay overnight.

Al and I had become pretty close by then. But I had also begun to figure out just where he was coming from. If Al found out where we were staying, he would always try to get there first to check where the best deal was, the best sleeping conditions, the room farthest away from the phone. He would try to secure for himself all the comforts of home, and whatever I got, well, that was the way it had to be. But this time, when we got down to the lodge, I had already beaten him to it. I had inspected the lodge first and gotten myself a nice bed. Al had to sleep on the couch. I loved it.

I got up the next morning and took a shower. The bathroom had one of those glass shower stalls. Suddenly someone knocked on the stall door. It was too fogged up to see, but I figured it was Al and hollered, "Wait 'til I get out of here. You get your shower next."

A woman's voice asked me if I was Mr. Packer, and I wondered what the hell was going on. She said there was a telephone call for me. I said, "Don't bother me. Al's in the other room. Get him to answer the phone."

"He said you should talk," she said.

"You tell him I'm in the shower and I'll be out in a second." She left, and I walked out with a towel wrapped around me. I asked Al why he hadn't picked up the phone.

"It's the people calling from New York, NBC," he said. "You talk to them."

I dried off and went over and picked up the phone. It was Scotty Connal on a conference call. All the key people from the network—Scotty, Chet Simmons, and Roy Hammerman, the key producing people—wanted to get our input on what games we thought were the best to televise. Immediately they got the wrong impression. They had called my room and a lady answered. They didn't know we weren't staying at a hotel and that the woman who answered the phone was Dick Wood's maid. They figured I was screwing around somewhere up in Michigan and not paying attention to the job. I was a little worried about that.

They started asking about the game, so I said, "Wait a minute. Al's right here with me. Let him get on the phone, too. There's no sense in my trying to give you all the answers."

And they said, "Al's there, too?" Right away they assumed that Al and I must really be rounders, both staying in the same room with a strange woman answering the phone. I got Al on and told him that Roy Hammerman, our producer, was on the line. Al called Roy Sunshine because Roy had moved to California. Al always has nicknames for people. He didn't know this was a conference call with all the key NBC people, so he got on the line and started yelling at Hammerman, "Sunshine, how the hell ya doin'?"

Of course the network brass was trying to make this a big serious conversation. It was still early enough in the game that the network people believed Al knew which the good matchups were. Al didn't even know which the good *teams* were. He didn't know them or the players. Secondly, the network people believed Al really cared. Mistake number two.

Now, I was really into it, just trying to think of which games would be good. And all the while Al was saying, "I can't believe these guys are bothering us here in Michigan."

We went down the lineup of tournament teams, and Al started playing with them a little bit, saying, "Oh, I tell you, that matchup between so and so, that's gonna be a hell of a game. Can't do without that one." Well, before we knew it, we had been on the phone 20 minutes, telling them that *all* the games were going to be good ones. And they were saying, "We better do that one. We can't miss this one or leave that one out. Al said it's a good one. Billy likes this one." Before we knew it, they had expanded the television coverage of the NCAA tournament to include just about every game.

When they got off the phone, Al started laughing and said, "I can't believe the decision to expand this tournament has taken place while we're lying here on this couch."

I say this with a bit of ego, but I really think that conversation had a lot to do with the growth of televised college basketball. Heaven forbid if we had said those games were going to be lousy.

During our first few years together, it became apparent that, although Dick, Al, and I worked together beautifully on the air and enjoyed each other socially, our personalities and interests were incredibly different.

Without question, Dick Enberg has everything in order. He does everything in a classy manner. He enjoys opera and New York plays and fine wines. He knows how to eat and dress properly and handles himself well in all social situations. He's just a high-caliber person. Traveling around with Al and me probably embarrassed Dick a great deal. I'm a middle-of-the-road person. I usually try to handle myself somewhat properly, but I don't have the background Dick has. Al sometimes looks more like a vagrant than he does a millionaire, but in most cases he travels pretty loosely. Dick enjoys eating good food in fine restaurants. Al avoids restaurants as much as possible and is more comfortable snacking on a hot dog. Once, while we were doing a game in New York, Dick planned to dine afterward at a fine French restaurant. But Al commandeered the limousine driver, and we wound up eating at Needick's hot dog stand. That type of situation was always developing on our trips. But we enjoyed each other's company and got to be close friends.

Dick had just experienced a very difficult marital separation and divorce. It had weighed on him heavily because he was a family man with a great deal of feeling for his wife and children. He often talked about them, sometimes so much that Al would get me off to the side and say, "I think Dick is getting too serious about this situation." One evening, Dick sat down with us and went through everything—the separation, his background, his entire story. How he had pushed himself to learn the trade of broadcasting at Indiana University, then worked in the trade briefly before heading west to become a teacher and coach at a California junior college.

Then Gene Autry discovered Dick Enberg's talents, and his career was again steered toward broadcasting. He made a rapid rise in radio and television, eventually working as a broadcaster for Autry's baseball team, the California Angels, and even doing a stint as a game show host. He was a workaholic during those years. His time was torn between doing Angels baseball and football for the Los Angeles Rams and UCLA in the Pac 10. Surely and steadily, Dick Enberg was becoming one of the prominent broadcasters in all of sports. CBS planned to hire him and brought him to New York to discuss a contract. Dick thought it was a terrific opportunity, with one exception: he felt obligated to Autry, who had given him his start. He went back to California and talked to Autry about this tremendous opportunity. Autry said, "Dick I'd really like to have you stay with me. It will give you the opportunity to stay here on the coast to enjoy your life and family. You'll only have to do X number of baseball games, and you can stop all this moonlighting. I'll match the offer with CBS."

Dick was delighted and went home to tell his wife. Instead, he discovered that their marriage had crumbled. She had someone else in her life. As Dick told us the story, we settled into melancholy and had a great deal of sympathy for him. We tried to find a way to ease him out of the conversation, away from the painful subject. But he was such a close and personal friend, and he seemed to need to tell his tale. In the end, Dick said he never could understand how his wife could have taken up with another man, especially a man who didn't wear nice clothes, wouldn't bathe, rode a motorcycle, and had long hair. As Dick spoke, I realized that Al was turning white.

Dick finished his story and left the table. When he had gone, I looked over at Al and said, "What was wrong?"

He said, "I'm just like the guy Dick was talking about. He couldn't see how anybody could possibly want to be with somebody like that. Somebody like me."

I said, "Oh, no, he's not talking about someone like you."

"Oh, yes he was," Al said. "He mentioned all the same characteristics I have. He likes to ride a motorcycle, he doesn't like to bathe, he wears sloppy clothes all the time, and he doesn't comb his hair. Who else could it be but a guy just like me? I hope Dick likes me a whole lot better than he likes that fella."

We went to Vegas for a game and stayed with one of Al's good friends, Morrie Jaeger, who manages the MGM Grand Casino. Even though the NBC people were staying at the Hilton, Morrie insisted that we stay with him at the MGM Grand. I had met Morrie in 1979 when the Final Four was in Salt Lake City.

Al had invited me to join him, Morrie, and a group of their friends at this restaurant that used to be an old monastery. Al had spoken so highly of Morrie and his friends that I was really looking forward to meeting them and going out for a good, relaxing meal. Al's wife, Pat, and his son, Rob, were there, as were Dick Enberg and Dick Wood. We had a group of about a dozen people. The restaurant managers put us at a huge banquet table. Everything had the makings of a very nice occasion.

About the time the salads got there, Al excused himself for a minute and left. I knew Al well enough to realize that we would probably not see him for a while. But I thought that, certainly since these were his friends, he could come back in a reasonable time. Normally he'd drift out and get a hamburger or a hot dog someplace and then come back when everybody was having dessert. He's a picky eater and doesn't eat much and never goes to a fine restaurant unless he's forced to or is getting paid to.

Well, that night we not only had our salads, but we ate our main course and had our desserts—and still no Al. Finally, the maitre d' came over and asked us if we knew the man asleep over in one of the booths. We couldn't see the booth from where we were sitting, but I knew what I'd find there. Sure enough, I walked over, and there he was, curled up in the booth, taking a nap in one of Salt Lake City's most fashionable restaurants. I guess he just got tired and thought it was time for a nap, just like John Riggins at the vice-president's speech. When it's time to nap, you just lie down and take a nap. The amazing thing about it was that no one in our group was surprised, including Al's wife, Pat, who just kind of shrugged her shoulders and said, "That's Al. We'll just wake him up when we're ready to leave, and he'll come with us."

After we finished dinner, we went over and got Al out of the booth and told him it was time to go. Without showing a trace of chagrin, he just sat up and said, "I hope everybody had a good time."

Morrie knew what he was in for when he invited us to stay at the MGM Grand. Al McGuire in Vegas? I figured it was time to look out. I wasn't very street smart and had no casino experience, so I decided to tail along while the others gambled. To tell the truth, I was eager to see my buddy Al absolutely razzle-dazzle everybody. I knew Al had to be the ınan who knew all about the gambling tables. I assumed Dick Enberg would be his typical self, very polite and meticulous, but lacking Al's ability to work the tables. Al was really fired up as we arrived at the airport. "Oh, boy, they better roll down their socks," he said. "I'm going to take them for everything they've got. Poor Morrie, I'm going to come in and clean out the house."

I thought, "Boy, I bet Al's out of sight when he gets into those card rooms." And Dick was very quiet. We got into the hotel and no more than got our bags upstairs in our room before we hit the crap tables. I stood back and watched Dick and Al play. Of course, Al was putting on a show for everybody, and Dick was reserved and cautious, just exactly as I had expected.

I kept an eye on my watch because we had to go to a production meeting at the other hotel, where the rest of the NBC crew was staying. They seemed to have great fun at the crap table, and everybody there was getting a tremendous kick out of Al McGuire and his Brooklynese. But when the time came around, I told them we had to leave.

"Come on, Dick, we've got to go," I said. Dick carefully counted his chips and got ready to leave. Al scooped up his and followed. There was an older lady playing at the table between Al and Dick. As we departed, she started screaming, "That man is taking my chips! He's taking my chips!"

I turned around and realized she was hollering at Al. I thought, "Oh, my goodness, calm that lady down." I went over and asked her, "Ma'am, what is it?"

"That crazy man," she shrieked, "he's been losing! I'm the one that's winning, and he's taking all my chips."

Al McGuire had faked out everybody. He had probably never played craps before in his life and didn't even know he was taking the other person's chips. He had no idea what he was betting on. He had taken the elderly woman's chips, and I had to take them from Al and give them back to the lady. Al said sheepishly, "I didn't know what I was doing, but I was having one hell of a good time."

Al has always enjoyed the speaking tour circuit. It's a big

part of his life because he likes to be on the road, meeting people and telling his stories over and over again. The big event our second year was a trip to French Lick, Indiana, Larry Bird's hometown. It was the spring of 1979, right after Larry had enjoyed a tremendous senior year at Indiana State. I wasn't held in high esteem in French Lick because I said Indiana State didn't really deserve to be number one in the country, because the team's schedule wasn't very difficult. Al McGuire, meanwhile, was the darling of the town. He said State deserved all the national attention.

I figured it would be fun to be in French Lick for Larry Bird's homecoming, so I didn't mind playing the bad guy. I met Al at the airport in Louisville, Kentucky. We were picked up there by some people from French Lick. Strangely, Al was on his finest behavior when those people met us, the best I had ever seen him with strangers. Very pleasant and talkative. I sat in the back seat, kind of amazed that he was so interested in talking with these people because normally he's rather nervous in these situations.

We drove to Jasper, Indiana, a town close to French Lick, and our escorts invited us into the home of some relatives. Al kissed the babies and kissed the grandmother and shook everybody's hand. He was just the most pleasant guy I had ever seen. I was kind of stunned, frankly. This wasn't the way Al normally acted when we went to speak somewhere. He usually wanted to be off by himself.

Then our escorts asked us if we'd like to meet other cousins. We went over to their house, and I watched Al go through the same routine. When we got back into the car, I really felt something was up. But I wasn't sure just what.

Then Al asked, ever so sweetly, "What about the cousin who's got the stained glass?"

At that point, I realized, "Uh-oh, there's the hit. Al's going to get himself some stained glass at the right kind of price." He's a collector of a number of things, and stained glass is one of his favorites. The people were overjoyed to take us over to this cousin's barn. We went in, and this fellow had an incredible collection of stained glass. Al looked at it, then turned to the rest of us and said, "Fellas, how about if you all go outside awhile while cousin Harry and I talk over the stained glass?"

We went outside, and I just started laughing to myself because poor cousin Harry was going to be missing some stained glass when this conversation was over. Sure enough, it wasn't long before Al came outside and said, "OK, fellas, I think everything is taken care of."

Then he turned back and said, "Harry, I want that stained glass shipped to Milwaukee. Make sure it's insured."

We got in the car and Al said, "That was terrific. Now look. When it comes time to pay me for the speech, just make sure that Harry gets paid for the stained glass and ship it up to me." Al had made a little trade, his speech for the stained glass. And that had made his day.

Our escorts, thrilled that Al had been so cordial, asked if he'd like to meet some more cousins. Al quickly said, "No, I've met everybody I want to meet today. Billy and I are tired now. How about taking us to the hotel?"

I just sat in the back seat and roared because Mr. McGuire had done it again.

Al may not have been good at picking up casino chips, but he's a deadeye when it comes to picking up speaking fees. One spring I got a call from McDonald's. I had been doing some work for their high school all-star game, and their public relations people wanted to know if I could bring Al along, too. They wanted Al to speak for them at a breakfast meeting of their owner/operators. I said, "I imagine Al would be interested in doing that." He and I were going to be getting together in Chicago anyway. They said the speaker's fee would be $2,500. I thought that was plenty and called Wanda, Al's secretary, and asked how much the coach needed to come down to Chicago to speak at a McDonald's breakfast. She said, "If you can get him $1,500, that would be OK."

"I can get him a little more than that," I said. "How about

$2,000?" I assumed that had Al covered. He'd never know I got the $500, although I'd give it to him later. I thought I'd get a kick out of fooling around with him there.

But when we got to the Hyatt House for the morning breakfast and Al saw all the people dressed in fine clothes, he looked at me and said, "This is no ordinary group we're meeting with. These are high rollers." Then he saw the sign, "Welcome Owner/Operators," and realized this was a major breakfast meeting for McDonald's. He said, "Hey, Billy, you'd better go find their people. I'm going to need some more money here. This kind of speech, you can run the price up on this. Go see the main man and see if I can get a little more."

I figured Wanda told him he was speaking for $1,500. So I said, "Well, Al, I got you $2,000."

"I think we can hit them up for $2,500 here," he said. Once again Mr. Street Smart was right on the money. He knew exactly how much they were willing to pay for that kind of breakfast. And he was worth every nickel of it. He went up and did a terrific job entertaining McDonald's owner/operators. In the process, he taught me another little lesson: Never try to con a con artist.

CHAPTER

7

BREAKING UP IS HARD TO DO

The 1980 NCAA Final Four was held in Indianapolis. There were two teams from the Big 10, Iowa and Purdue, plus Larry Brown's UCLA team, which had shocked everybody. They had struggled throughout the tournament, compared to the way UCLA teams approached the tournament during Wooden's years. The fourth team, the only truly excellent club in the group, was Louisville. Without question, it was not one of the best fields. The other three teams were overachievers.

As usual, the Final Four was a mass of news media, all focused on the four teams and their coaches. Added to that, as it is each year, was the coaches' convention, which created even more of a stir. The whole event becomes a giant center of news and gossip about the past, present, and future of college basketball. All that competition makes it tough for network announcers to come up with a unique story. It's very hard to scoop anybody with all the talented reporters around. But through a friendship with the Louisville team manager, I had learned of a human interest piece about Wiley Brown,

Louisville's center, a mountain of a guy who played professional football after leaving college. Wiley didn't have a thumb on one hand, but he wore a prosthesis, a plastic thumb that enabled him to handle the ball. Unfortunately, Wiley, while eating the pregame meal before the championship, had taken off his thumb and put it on the table. And when he finished eating, he forgot and left his thumb there. After the team left, the busboys had cleaned up the tables, putting all the scraps and Wiley's thumb in the garbage. Once Wiley realized what he had done, team officials sent the manager back to look for the thumb. You can imagine how Denny Crum felt, playing for the National Championship and his starting center without a thumb. But after sifting through the garbage, the manager found Wiley's thumb. And I had a scoop.

Now, normally, the eccentric and off-the-wall stories like that were Al's beat, even though I would try to scoop him whenever I could. The trick was to keep the story a secret from each other until we got on the air, and then we'd go for the surprise reaction. So I was real proud of the Wiley Brown story. I figured it was a winner, and I couldn't wait to throw it on McGuire sometime during the game. A thumb in the garbage was the kind of thing Al could turn into an hour-long dissertation and the fact that Al didn't know about it made me so happy I couldn't stand it.

Finally, the right moment arrived, and I threw the story out. "You're not going to believe what happened today," I began and proceeded to tell it. I expected a tremendous reaction from Dick and Al. But my story was so outlandish, Al simply commented to Dick that I was nuts. And Dick really put me down, suggesting I was off on a tangent and implying, "Hey, this is the National Championship game. Don't make up a story now." And, of course, Al didn't believe it was true either, but nonetheless, he came up with one of the classic comments of all time:

"Well," Al said, "that waitress sure got a hell of a tip."

In 1980–81, we did an early-season game between Indiana

and North Carolina at Chapel Hill. The evening before the game, Dean Smith invited Al and me to go to dinner with him. We had watched Carolina practice that afternoon, a ritual that helps broadcasters prepare background information for the game the next day. Although Al doesn't like to go to fancy restaurants and seldom likes to talk basketball when we're on the road, he and I agreed to dinner because Dean is such a fine host and gentleman.

I had not yet checked into the hotel, and I told Al that my son, Mark, and I would go back to check in and would meet Dean and Al at the restaurant. After checking in, we went to the restaurant and found four people—Dean; Al; Carolina's sports information director, Rick Brewer; and another person, whom I'll leave unnamed for the moment. They were seated in the special dining room Dean had set up for the evening. Mark and I sat down, and we ordered a few drinks and hors d'oeuvres. As expected, the conversation turned to basketball, and everybody was taking part, particularly the unnamed fellow at the end of the table. Finally, after a few minutes of conversation, Al looked down at the person and said, "Fella, I don't know you. What do you do for a living?"

Dean Smith looked surprised, and we all kind of laughed. Al, taken aback momentarily, said, "No, seriously, I don't believe I've ever seen you before. What do you do? You seem to know quite a bit about basketball."

At that point, Dean Smith introduced Al to the fellow at the end of the table, who happened to be Bob Costas, our NBC broadcast partner for the game the next day. Bob had been unable to get to the practices because his plane ran late. And Al, who never watches any television, certainly hadn't recognized Bob Costas. So I wasn't surprised that Al didn't know him. But everybody else at the table thought Al was joking because he certainly would have to know a commentator of Costas's ability. Bob, who is recognized today as one of the finest broadcasters in the business, will probably never forget that first meeting with Al.

That somewhat rough introduction was followed by an interesting broadcast the next day. In fact, Bob and Al spent a little more time together than either anticipated. First, we went on the air a little bit early. Then, Bobby Knight's team wasn't playing too well, while Dean Smith's club was well tuned. Of course, both teams would meet again in the National Championship game in Philadelphia, when the tables would be turned. But in this early game, the Tar Heels got control in the second half. Not only did they have control, but Smith sent them into their famed four-corner offense. Rather than get into a situation where he would commit fouls, Bobby Knight held back his Indiana team and allowed time to run off the clock. Realizing this and being very familiar with the Carolina system, I saw that this game was going to be over in a hurry, and I asked our producer, Ken Edmondson, how much time we were going to have to fill. The bad news: about 35–40 minutes. A broadcaster's nightmare.

And the action on the floor wasn't helping. Carolina's slowdown four-corner offense was actually speeding things up because Indiana wasn't doing anything to stop it. Quickly, we decided that it would be best for me to head down on the floor with significant time remaining in the game to work on lining up a number of interviews. That way we could fill the time slot. I went to the floor knowing the interviews would be long and drawn out and probably not very entertaining, but it was the best we could do, given the situation.

As predicted, the game did end very early. Well, we interviewed a whole range of Carolina players, past and present, plus the coaches, the cheerleaders, everybody. I would interview a few people and then throw it back up to Bob and Al to recap a little bit while I organized my next interview. Unfortunately, Bob Costas was still a bit awed by Al McGuire, who still had the attitude that his work was finished at the buzzer. After the game, Al's mind starts to wander to other things. The first time I threw it back up, Bob gave a concise report of the game and then threw it to Al by saying, "What a terrific day for Dudley Bradley, our Chevrolet Most Valuable Player."

Al looked at him and said, "You've got to be kidding. Bradley Dudley [Al always reversed the guy's name] couldn't have been the MVP. It had to have been Al Wood." Now, normally, Bob Costas would have known who was the MVP; he has an almost photographic memory for game statistics and names. But Al seemed so sure of himself that Bob said, "Oh, that's right, Al. It's Al Wood." Then they threw it back to me, which allowed me to correct them. I started kidding them: "Hey, we still have a long way to go on this telecast, and, guys, we did pick Dudley Bradley as our MVP."

Finally, we got the MVP straight and proceeded to fill up the hour. Our final interview that day, making it obvious that we were really reaching, was with James Worthy's father. Worthy, who now plays for the Los Angeles Lakers, resembles his father greatly. So I interviewed Mr. Worthy on the angle "Can anyone out in the audience determine who this man is?" We spent the last few minutes of the broadcast dragging it out with an introduction of Mr. Worthy. I just kept hoping that our viewers had either departed during the closing minutes of the runaway game or gone to sleep during the postgame show.

To this day, Al and I kid about Bobby Costas. Bob isn't tall, and at that first Carolina game, it was difficult for him to see the floor from our perch in the press box at Carmichael Auditorium. So he sat on some telephone books to see. Since Al can never remember his name, he always calls him "Yellow Pages." Al recognizes Bob Costas for what an outstanding announcer he is, but he can never resist the urge to hang a name on someone.

As strangely as that season started, it continued and finally ended just as strangely.

First, it would turn out to be the last time that Dick, Al, and I would work together on television. At the time, we had no idea we were finished as a broadcast team: our thoughts were turned to the championship game between Indiana and Carolina in Philadelphia's Spectrum. And we were pretty upset that our network, NBC, would not be carrying the National Championship for the next three years. CBS had gotten the rights to the Final Four for a while.

When we received news of that, Dick, Al, and I were furious. We would miss the championships for '82, '83, and '84. All of us, especially Al, pushed for a meeting with the network's top executives to work out a strategy to get the championship back. Unfortunately, that meeting was postponed a number of times, and it became obvious to all of us that the network executives saw no reason for us to get involved. But finally, at the Final Four in Philadelphia, we had our meeting.

We sat down with the NBC Sports top brass—Don Ohlmeyer, executive producer; Arthur Watson, president; and Don Wear, vice-president for negotiations—and discussed company policy. But as the conversation began, Al got up and walked away from the table. Nobody paid much attention, but I was a little worried. I couldn't imagine why he was so uninterested, especially after he had worked so hard to set up this meeting.

He walked over to a bank of six or seven telephones in the hotel room where we were meeting. One by one, he took them off the hook, and within seconds all of them were making that horrible buzzing noise that phones make when they're left off the hook. Everybody looked up, and Al realized he had our attention.

"There's no way we can have a meeting that's this important with this many phones in the room," he said, "because surely as soon as we get into something important, one of these phones is going to ring. As typical executives, you'll get up to answer it, and that will delay the meeting. If we're going to get anything done, let's either go to another room without phones or leave these off the hook."

He had made a clear point; if we're going to have a meeting, let's concentrate and get something accomplished. The meeting proceeded, but even without interruptions it didn't lead to anything solid. At the time, the NBC people were rather confident that they would have a chance to get the Final Four contract back. They thought CBS would have a hard time fulfilling a part of the contract that called for the network to broadcast regular-season games. The NBC people thought they had the regular season locked up, because of the deal they had arranged through TVS, Eddie Einhorn's company. Their contract with TVS gave them control of the games in most major conferences around the country. The NBC Sports people figured that, when the NCAA learned that CBS couldn't get the rights to regular season games, the contract would be rescinded. And NBC would again have the Final Four.

As we now know, it didn't quite work out that way. CBS was able to piece together a regular-season schedule for two years, until the NBC/TVS exclusive rights to the major conferences ran out. Not only was CBS able to hold on to the contract for three years; it was also able to negotiate an extension for another three. But I'm getting ahead of my story.

Although the meeting didn't produce results, we couldn't do much about it at the time. There were more pressing matters—we still had the Final Four to broadcast. That in itself would be quite a challenge. In retrospect, I'm glad we didn't know then that it would be our last broadcast together. If we had, the mood would have been very somber. And the circumstances were already difficult.

The Sunday before the Monday night championship game was a typical Final Four day, filled with meetings and media events. When Monday came, I got away by myself to prepare for the broadcast, the culmination of the long college basketball season. I spent my time alone, thinking about all the factors of a Carolina-Indiana rematch. So many things had changed since the two teams met earlier. Bobby Knight's team was on a real high. And for the first time in a while, the University of North Carolina would be facing a National Championship game with a healthy team. In years past, Dean Smith's teams would make it to the finals only to be hindered by injuries. Still, I really sensed that Indiana had the momentum. I spent a great deal of time that morning and afternoon thinking of the previous meetings between those two great teams. Smith held a 2-0 win streak over Knight. And, if anything, Bobby Knight is competitive.

I arranged the facts I needed for the game and headed over to the Spectrum. Just as I got out of my car, someone mentioned that President Reagan had been shot. I realized I must have really been out of it that afternoon because that was the first I'd heard of it, although it had happened a few hours before. I hurried to the TV truck and there found Al, Dick, and Don Ohlmeyer, who was a guy with the ability to handle a crisis. He has a great sense of command. Immediately the question had arisen: Would NBC broadcast the game with the president in grave danger? In the earliest reports, there was no indication of the president's condition. NBC would have to make its decisions as the news developed. To get organized for whatever would happen, Don called on Bryant Gumbel, who by that time had become a superstar at NBC Sports, hosting the major events, including NFL football and the NCAA championship. I was pleased to see Bryant's career advancement—now, of course, he's the co-host of the "Today Show." Along his path to the top, Bryant had earned the respect of everyone in the business. And the challenges he faced on that day of the championship showed why.

Ohlmeyer, Gumbel, Enberg, Al, and I all huddled together to discuss the problems. To be quite honest, although Al and I listened carefully to what Ohlmeyer had to say, we were figuring that the game would be played the next day. We began thinking about what effect moving the game would have on the teams and players. Ohlmeyer, Gumbel, and Enberg, however, were all business. Don asked all four of us to write out any comments we might make on the air regarding the president should the news be bad. Bryant and Dick did that, but Al and I didn't worry about it. We figured that, if the game was aired that night, NBC's news professionals could handle any commentary on the president's shooting and we'd keep our minds as best we could on basketball.

The situation left Ohlmeyer and the sports staff in a tough

situation. Here it was, one of the major sporting events of the year, and the decision to broadcast it was going down to the wire. Then Wayne Duke, Big 10 Commissioner and head of the NCAA basketball committee, made a tough but logical decision: the game would be played if President Reagan was out of danger. That meant tournament officials would wait until the very last minute to decide whether to send the teams out for early practice 25 minutes prior to tip-off.

Finally, word came that President Reagan was out of danger. The NCAA decided to play the game, but since news about the shooting was still breaking, Ohlmeyer wasn't sure how much time he would have for the lead into the broadcast. The situation revealed just how professional the NBC staff was, particularly the director, the technical people, Enberg, and Gumbel. Bryant had spent three or four hours putting together opening lines for the introduction to the game. He had been told he would have two to three minutes at the top of the show to set the tone properly for the broadcast. But as we were ready to begin, word came down that Bryant's two or three minutes would be chopped to no more than 45 seconds. With no problem at all, Bryant trimmed his opening and gave a great performance that night. His comments were perfect, putting the situation in the proper perspective for the audience. He said that, although this was the game for the National Championship, much more had transpired during the course of the day, and fortunately for all, President Reagan was out of danger.

I've often wondered what it was like in the dressing rooms of the two teams that night. Dean Smith and Bobby Knight are two of the top coaches in all of college basketball, each with very distinct personalities: Knight, a man of emotion and intensity; Smith, a believer in organization, calm, and understanding. It was perhaps the toughest for the players, young men trying to prepare for the biggest game of their lives, yet not knowing until the last minute whether or not it would even be played.

The most memorable thing about the night, however, was the little lesson in network power. NBC didn't tell the NCAA what to do. Wayne Duke made his decision to play the game without any input from the network. And that's the way it should be.

After the season ended, I turned my thoughts in the spring of 1981 to the dismal realization that NBC wouldn't be doing the NCAA championship anymore, and I centered my attention on doing whatever I could to help NBC maintain its position in collegiate basketball.

I got a phone call one morning from Don Ohlmeyer, much to my surprise because he had never called me before. Don said that it was very important that NBC be on top of Ralph Sampson's decision about whether to go pro following his sophomore year. Sampson had been a major story every spring after he finished the basketball season, as the sports world waited to see whether he would turn pro. His freshman year, the big story was Ralph's meeting with Red Auerbach and the controversy that surrounded his decision to stay in school. It seemed that every year the story got bigger and bigger.

Ohlmeyer said, "Billy, I want you to go to Charlottesville, Virginia, right away and get the Sampson story. CBS is sending a crew of people in there, and we've got to get the story over CBS. This is extremely important to us, and I want to be on top of it."

"Well, gee," I said, "today's only Monday and Ralph doesn't have to decide until Saturday. Why don't I just call Ralph up and ask him?

Ohlmeyer said, "You've got to be kidding. Nobody can get to Ralph Sampson. You've got to go up there."

I told him I'd known Ralph a long time, and one of the things I'd always treasured about being involved in collegiate athletics was that I'd established a degree of honesty and integrity with the ball players. Over the years, I've established good friendships. I think the players understand that, when I do a game, I try to be honest about their good and bad points.

In any case, I told Ohlmeyer, I think I have established a

good rapport with Ralph, and I felt very confident that I could call him up, ask him a question, and I was sure Ralph would get back to me with an honest answer.

I told Don I would be happy to take this assignment, but I wanted to do it my way. If I didn't get the proper information, then he could feel free to put anybody on the story he wanted.

Don said, "You do it any way you want to; it's all right with me. But you better get the damn story."

What amazes me about network television people is their affinity for secrecy and intrigue. If they can make something difficult by sending camera crews and whatnot to stake out news stories, they'll do it every time.

So I called Ralph and said, "Look, NBC would like to get the story. We've covered your games. It's extremely important that our network have an opportunity to get your decision first. I'd like to get the story from you, but I don't want to infringe on your decision-making process. All I'm asking of you is, when you know what you're going to do, that you let me know because I'd like to come up there and do an interview with you so I can get it to NBC."

Ralph said, "Billy, I don't know what I'm going to do yet. I've got a lot of thinking to do in the next couple of days. I appreciate your calling me, and I can assure you that I'll call you up when I know what I'm going to do."

I thanked him, gave him my number, and hung up. I got a call the next day from Ohlmeyer's office stating that they knew CBS had sent an entire crew, including a TV radar dish, down to Charlottesville to camp out. Ohlmeyer wanted to know when I was going to make my move to Charlottesville. I told them that I'd talked to Ralph and that he would let me know when he was ready. I don't think the people in New York thought I was too interested or even capable of getting this story because I obviously had not gone to Charlottesville to camp out with Ralph Sampson. Well, by about 9 or 10 o'clock on Friday night, I'll admit I was getting a little nervous. I thought, Ralph's going to let me down; he's not going to let me know.

Finally, Ralph called at about 10 o'clock and said, "Billy, I've decided what I'm going to do. Could you come up here on Saturday morning? I'd be happy to meet with you and get this story for NBC."

I called NBC and told the producers not to send a crew down to Charlottesville because I wanted to prove to NBC that there was always overkill in the equipment and people they moved around to get stories. Instead, I called the local TV station in Charlottesville and told the manager, "Hey, look, I'm going to be in Charlottesville tomorrow morning. I would like to borrow your crew, and I'd be willing to pay $150 for the crew to do a little segment with Ralph Sampson."

The manager said, "Billy, if you'll do an interview with us, we'll send the crew over for free, and we'll just give you the tapes."

I felt great about that. I was getting the piece done, and it wasn't going to cost NBC a dime. CBS had been camped out there with people and radar dishes for a week, and I had scooped 'em. At that point in my life, CBS was the enemy.

I flew to Charlottesville and went over to the gymnasium where Ralph had told me to meet him in Terry Holland's office. I walked into the gymnasium, and Terry Holland, who walked in a few minutes behind me, said, "What are you doing here?"

"Well," I said, "I'm here because Ralph called me and told me to come on in. He's ready to make his decision."

Terry said, "Well, gee, when did he call?"

"He called at about 10:30," I said.

"I think he called me at about 11:00," Terry said.

I thought that was kind of comical, but I certainly didn't want to put myself between Ralph and Terry. But Ralph, being the high-quality guy he was, had really kept his word.

"We've got some problems here," Terry said. "CBS wants to do the interview, and we have decided that Ralph is not going to appear before anybody for a personal interview. I hope you understand that. We're going to have him go over to the university TV station, where he's going to make his statement. Then we'll provide tapes for everybody who would like to have one."

I said, "Terry, that'd be great with me because NBC goes on the air with a baseball game in Baltimore at about one, and I'd sure like to have that tape to take along so they could air it at the baseball game."

He said, "I'm sure we can get it for you."

I never did get to see Ralph face to face that day. I left a note for him saying that I appreciated his honesty with me. I got the tape, got back on the plane, flew to Baltimore, and delivered the tape to the TV truck there. We aired the announcement on the pregame show of the NBC baseball "Game of the Week," and obviously caught everybody else with their pants down.

CBS still had a crew in Charlottesville, Virginia, refusing to take the tape that the university did and causing Terry Holland a great deal of concern. They were camped out on Holland's lawn with camera equipment, and his wife was very upset about it. I knew that they had spent upwards of $10-11,000 to have that crew and all that equipment there, and yet we were able to beat them on the air.

When I got home, I found out that Isiah Thomas and Mark Aguirre had decided to go pro. Then, the next morning, I read in the newspaper that Buck Williams, the great University of Maryland player, had also decided to go into the NBA. It gave me the idea for a story. I called Ohlmeyer, who was pretty pleased with the way the Sampson story turned out, and told him I wanted to do a piece for "Sports World" on the difference between Sampson's decision-making process and that of the three others who had decided to turn pro. He said, if I thought it was a good idea, go right ahead.

I was all excited, so the first thing I did was call up Bobby Knight to ask if I could contact Isiah directly. I did that as a courtesy to Bob: even though Isiah was going pro, he was still a member of the Indiana basketball team, and I wouldn't want to go behind the coach's back. Unfortunately, Bobby had been out of town, and he still didn't know that Isiah was leaving school. Bobby was upset, and after we hollered at each other for a couple of minutes, he said, "Hell, if you want to talk to Isiah, feel free to do so. Nothing is going to change at this point. Yeah, feel free to get in touch with Isiah. I've got no hard feelings."

I thought how strange it was: here's Bobby Knight coaching a national championship team, Isiah is his key ball player, and they really hadn't even discussed his decision. I called Isiah and asked to interview him. Isiah was always a captivating interview; he has a sparkle in his eye, one of the best personalities I've covered in college basketball.

But this time, Isiah was hesitant and said, "Billy, I can't talk about that now without talking to my agent." I didn't even realize that he must have had that agent before the Saturday deadline, which, in effect, was illegal.

About an hour later, I got a call from George Andrews of Chicago, who, with his brother Harold, operates one of the most successful agenting groups in the United States. They represent both Isiah and Mark Aguirre, as well as Magic Johnson and others, and have done a tremendous job for all of their clients. I told them I'd like to interview Mark and Isiah about why they decided to turn pro. They established some guidelines and told me to come to Chicago, but they wanted to be present when I did the interview with Mark and then go down to Bloomington, Indiana, with me to interview Isiah. "We want to make sure it doesn't get out of line, and if it does get out of line, we want the right to step in and put a stop to it," they said.

I said that seemed perfectly fair to me and set up a time for the interview. Then I called Ray Meyer, told him I was coming to Chicago, and said I wanted to talk to him about what it meant to lose a player of Aguirre's style, what it all meant for college basketball. Ray said he'd be happy to do it. He had to speak at Bradley University but would come back to do the interview with me that afternoon after the speech.

I set up a rather rigorous day, talking with Mark Aguirre in the morning in Chicago, Ray Meyer right after lunch, and then Isiah down in Bloomington, Indiana. At that time, Isiah was in the middle of exams, but he had arranged to be free that evening. Then I got in touch with Lefty Driesell, who was really hot over what had happened with Buck Williams, but I knew my rapport with Buck and Lefty would help me line them up for a third interview. My idea was to talk to these players about what factors they had weighed in deciding to turn pro. For some reason, I thought the coaches and players had spent a great deal of time discussing the matter, and I wanted to get the bottom line.

I called NBC to set up things for Chicago, but met with some resistance. The network people at first said they didn't know why they should go to Chicago but then agreed after I explained about the interviews I had set up. I was told Hillary Cosell, Howard Cosell's daughter, would be the producer of the piece. I had never before worked with Hillary Cosell or anybody else from her department.

When I met the crew at O'Hare airport, I found that the crew really wasn't prepared. There was no time to rent a car, so we had to pile into a cab. And Hillary Cosell showed up wearing a satin baseball jacket, a pair of blue jeans rolled up to her knees, and a pair of socks with multicolored stripes. She was also chewing gum. I was already annoyed, and now I was really embarrassed. That's not the way we show up to do ball games or interviews, and it was obvious that Hillary was not too interested in the story I wanted to do.

When we got out to DePaul, George and Harold Andrews, Mark, and I headed for a little hot dog shop to talk and make sure that we were all on the same wavelength. I explained my point of view for the story, and they were very happy about my approach. All of a sudden, Hillary Cosell walks into the hot dog shop, sits down beside us, and rudely introduces herself, taking the approach that she's the producer of the show and here's the way it's going to work. This made us all very uncomfortable, but George and Harold had the presence of mind to say, "OK, let's go forward with it."

Things went downhill from there. I hadn't interviewed Mark Aguirre before and didn't realize that his media exposure had given him a streetwise ability to manipulate his questioners. He had his line down very well, and I didn't know what Mark was honestly thinking because he was a super con man. I started to ask questions and quickly realized that the interview would be very flat. Mark seemed to have rehearsed his comments about how much he enjoyed playing at DePaul, how playing in the NBA was something he had always dreamed of, that it was a tremendous opportunity for him, even though he would miss his teammates.

I continued probing, trying to get some real information from him, but I did not do a good job at all. Much to the satisfaction of Hillary, it turned out that we really had nothing. I thanked Mark and George and Harold for what they had done and asked Mark to have lunch with Coach Meyer and me. Mark declined and said he hadn't seen his coach in a while, which I thought was kind of strange, since I assumed he and Meyer had talked extensively about this important decision.

After the meeting, Hillary came over to inform me that there would be no Ray Meyer interview because what we'd gotten from Mark Aguirre wasn't worthy of being on television. I was very upset. I said, "Wait a minute. Ray Meyer is flying all the way back to DePaul, and we're supposed to meet him at one o'clock. There's no way I can stop him now. Besides, I'm supposed to meet Isiah Thomas after exams out in Bloomington."

She said, "Well, we're not doing the interviews with either one of them. You've got no story here."

It wasn't that I didn't agree with her about the story, but I was angered at her seeing no reason to be courteous to the people we had asked to stand by for the interviews. I said, "No, we're going to do the interview with Ray Meyer. I don't even care if you don't put tape in the machine; we're going to do it. I'll call Isiah and cancel out with him. But with Ray going out of his way to fly back here to help us out, we are going to interview Ray Meyer." I was stern enough about it that, while it annoyed Hillary, she agreed that we would go down to the coach's office and do the taping at one o'clock.

Ray showed up exactly on time, and when he walked through the door I was on the phone with Isiah, telling him that we were not coming to Bloomington. Isiah, as usual, was kidding around with me, saying, "Billy, I never believed that you would come."

I said, "Gee, Isiah, I said I was coming, and I appreciate what you've done."

He said, "No, you only want to talk to the big stars. Now that you've got Mark Aguirre done, you don't need me. I never thought you guys were coming to do a guy like me. That's OK, though. Someday I'm going to prove to you that I'm really going to be a star in basketball."

He was really pulling my chain, but I appreciated his attitude, considering I had put him through so much trouble. Just as Ray came in the door, I said, "Hey, Coach, I've got a kid on the phone that's a pretty good player. And he just told me that, if he doesn't make it in the pros, he'd like to come back and finish out his eligibility in his hometown of Chicago, if you have any use for him."

Then I put Ray on the phone with Isiah. They started kidding back and forth, and Ray was laughing. You could tell that Isiah was also having a good time talking to Ray. They had a very relaxed rapport.

When Ray hung up, I asked him about the problems a coach faces when a superstar is considering turning pro and what that does to a ball club. Ray got very emotional about it and talked about how it had totally destroyed his opportunity as a coach to work with players. He said that the agents were getting to the players to the extent that a coach could never really know what was going on in a kid's mind and that it was very difficult for a coach. He had been very close to Mark as a freshman and a sophomore, but then, all of a sudden, Mark started to pull away. Through the junior year, a gap appeared in the player-coach relationship. Ray said it was one of the most difficult things he had experienced as a coach. We're talking about a guy who's been in the business for 40 years.

Right away, I thought, "Wait a second. Here he's just gotten off the phone with Isiah Thomas, and they spoke as if they were great friends." Bobby Knight and Isiah had not talked, yet Bobby was Isiah's coach. And Mark Aguirre and Ray hadn't talked at all. I realized then that Mark didn't want to face Ray that afternoon. That's why he didn't go to lunch with us: he didn't want to see his coach. I said, "Ray, when was the last time you and Mark sat down and discussed that situation?"

He said, "We really haven't talked for a long time. We separated; we parted. And it hurts, because you would like to be a part of that decision-making process. But what happens is the player is told that, if he goes to the coach for the answers, the coach will have reason to tell him to stay in school. Therefore, the gap widens every day."

Right then I realized that my story had nothing to do with why these guys decided to go or why Ralph Sampson decided to stay. The story should explore the system of the hardship draft and how it has created a tremendous gap in coach-player relationships. The decision to turn pro becomes a destructive factor in a positive relationship that coach and player should cherish. I really got excited about pursuing that story, knowing that Bobby and Isiah, Ray and Mark, Lefty and Buck had all broken off their relationships.

After I finished the interview with Ray, I told Hillary about this new angle on the story. Well, she didn't see much point in that story. She wouldn't go down to Bloomington, but she *would* take the interviews we had to New York and let me know. I really thought I was onto something very solid, so I was really disappointed when I got a call from Don Ohlmeyer's office stating that I might have a little something there, but they didn't see a place for it on "Sports World," and they'd get back to me later. They never did; those pieces of tape were never used. I was never allowed to get the story of the breakdown of Isiah Thomas and Bobby Knight, which to this day is still not a close relationship. The story of Buck Williams and Lefty Driesell was even more interesting in that Buck was actually kept away from Lefty the night that he made his decision. Lefty couldn't get to him. And when the NBA held its draft, the players went one, two, three: Aguirre, Thomas, Williams. But the story was never used.

I didn't realize it then, but this incident was part of the reason that I decided to look into the situation at CBS a few months later. That little episode reinforced my attitude that "Hey, there is no way to fight the system. Maybe there's a better system somewhere else."

I had no real desire to leave NBC. In fact, I thought the future of our broadcast team looked great, despite the fact that NBC had lost the Final Four contract. We had discussed the things we would like to do to promote basketball. Dick, Al, and I had become close friends, and although the three of us hadn't done much as business partners, we felt comfortable with each other in both business and social situations. Anything we did, we did with a handshake.

I presented the NBC executives with a package of things that Dick, Al, and I could do to help the network compete with CBS. First, I wanted to see NBC put together a preseason basketball publication, filled with slick editorial copy on each region, rather than the basic reports that most basketball yearbooks offer. NBC would lend support through promotions and publicity. I asked for no money because I believed we could finance the thing through advertising. Second, I thought our threesome could get involved in a college basketball radio show. Third, I thought my expertise would be helpful to the network in arranging a schedule that would shut CBS out of most of the major regular-season games. With two networks in tough competition, we needed to turn to competitive scheduling. With a better schedule, NBC would share in the revenue and exposure of college ball. I also thought that our threesome could produce halftime shows and features and package them for the network. I suggested something much along the lines of what NBC does today with "On the Road with Al McGuire."

Along with those concepts, I included the idea of forming a network speaker's bureau, featuring NBC's great collection of talent. I wasn't asking for money to initiate these projects. We would underwrite them personally, yet perform them under the supervision of NBC. The income generated would be ours, and there would be no risk to the network.

When I first presented these ideas, both orally and in writing, I was met with a tremendous amount of enthusiasm. However, when I asked the NBC people to put their enthusiasm in writing, they resisted and said basically that they wanted me to be a broadcaster and not worry about these other things. "Let's just finalize your agreement as a broadcaster," they said, "and we'll worry about the other things later."

Almost right after that meeting, I got a call from Dick Stockton, who had been a friend and a fellow broadcaster at NBC and who had moved over to CBS. Dick and I had known each other since the days we broadcast Carolina Cougar/American Basketball Association games together. He told me that the sports executives at CBS were undecided about what they were going to do for a color man for their basketball broadcasts and that they were also concerned about finding a play-by-play man. I told Dick that I had never thought about leaving NBC, but if CBS was interested, I saw no reason why it couldn't be a possibility.

Dick set up a meeting for me with Kevin O'Malley and Van Gordan Sauter of CBS Sports. I set up a meeting for myself with NBC. In fact, both meetings were held on the same day. I flew to New York and met with Van Sauter and O'Malley in the morning and outlined to them some of the things I would like to do in addition to broadcasting with CBS. I wanted the network to use my expertise in areas of scheduling, marketing, and potential sales or production ideas. Basically, I wanted to play a role in the development of the college basketball package. The meeting was very cordial, very businesslike, and very well organized.

Then I went over to NBC. I was disturbed that four months had gone by and still nothing had been put in writing that guaranteed my position and the opportunity to pursue my ideas. Instead, the NBC people were incredibly preoccupied with whether I had the authority to represent Dick Enberg and Al McGuire on business matters. I told them I really didn't need any authority, that we were friends, that we wanted to pursue these ideas, and that we would work out our side of the bargain without any trouble. Obviously, I felt a great amount of resistance on the part of NBC to go along with any of the ideas that I had outlined, and to be quite honest, I was upset that so much time had been wasted. The meeting broke down without anything being accomplished.

Three days later, I received a letter from CBS, defining exactly and precisely what we had discussed at the meeting and exactly what CBS would like my role to be. They were encouraging me to be involved in their new production of college basketball in any degree I wanted.

NBC, on the other hand, sent a one-page letter that didn't give much hope that we would ever reach an agreement regarding the ideas I had presented months before. And it took only a minute for me to decide to go to CBS. We hadn't even talked about money, but I wasn't really concerned. If I had the opportunity to work the way I wanted to, the money would take care of itself.

About a week later, I sat down with CBS and reached an agreement without any problems. And I haven't looked back since. I miss my association with Dick and Al and the many years I spent with NBC. But obviously, things have worked out very well with CBS. To this day, the people there have been great to work with.

The CBS people offered me the opportunity to be in the total design of their college basketball broadcasts—broadcasting, sales, promotion—the whole works. That arrangement has kept my varied interests challenged. Still, over the past few years, I've missed working with Dick and Al. Sometimes, when we see each other, we talk about getting back together, even if just for one broadcast. And someday, I'd really like to see that happen.

CHAPTER

8

RIVALRIES

Al and I put our pride on the line and coached against each other in a series of college All-Star games. You know the type; they're supposed to be all fun without much emphasis on the competition. Fat chance.

The first time we matched wits was in North Carolina, where a friend, Neal McGeachy, put together postseason All-Star games, pitting the best players from the ACC against each other. He asked Al and me to coach against each other. I thought it would be a lot of fun and a great opportunity for Al and his wife, Pat, to come down and stay with Barbara and me for a while. So we agreed.

The first night, Al had the superior team, with Carolina stars Michael O'Koren and Dudley Bradley, whom Al always calls Bradley Dudley. I had players from Wake Forest and a few other schools. There was a sellout crowd in the Winston-Salem Coliseum. I was really looking forward to just having fun. I didn't realize that Al wanted to prove I couldn't coach and he still had the magic wand.

Al got stuck that night because some of his players weren't

in the best shape and didn't make the required effort. For them, it was just an exhibition game, not a matter of life or death. My kids, on the other hand, seemed to try a little harder. The game was close the first half, but we won rather handily. To me, the game was no big deal. But then I realized Al was really upset by the loss. I learned that night he was really primed for the rematch the next day in Charlotte. But when we got to Charlotte, it appeared that two of Al's key players, O'Koren and Al Wood, wouldn't be there.

Al stormed into my dressing room and said, "Hey, we've got to swap some players here. You've got the superior team." So he took a couple of my players and left me with fellows like Frank Johnson and Larry Nance, who have become outstanding NBA players but who were just seniors then. I thought that was only fair. We were trying to entertain the fans and needed balanced teams. Then, five minutes before we sent the teams onto the floor, Al sent my two players back. They came back into the dressing room and said Wood and O'Koren had shown up and Al decided he didn't need my guys after all. They also said that Al was really fired up in the locker room, telling his guys they had to win. I said, "Well, hell, if he's going to take things that seriously, then I think it would be a good idea for us to go out there and really try to rip his team."

Which is exactly what we did. In no short order, we got them down by about 20 points. I took the opportunity to give Al a real rough time on the sidelines, goading him at every point. He got really angry. As a matter of fact, we were going out to eat that night, but after the game, he wouldn't even speak to me. He left the arena and wouldn't appear on TV or anything. It had really gotten to him. He tries to give the impression that he doesn't miss coaching, but when he gets into the arena, he's all business.

He got a shot at a rematch when we coached an All-Star game at Cedar Rapids, Iowa, in 1983. It was supposed to be a game between the best of the Big 10 and ACC senior classes. Dick Enberg was to do the play-by-play with Bobby Knight as color analyst. It turned out to be a first-class affair. Al and I were primed to compete again.

When I arrived at the arena, Al's Big 10 team was already working out. I asked the people in charge where my team was. They had only three ACC players there, and all three of them had been substitutes. So I asked, "When are you expecting the rest of the players?"

"We hope that some more come in," they said. "You should have five by game time [the next day]."

"That's ridiculous," I said. "You can't have an All-Star game with five players on one team."

Al had a real strong squad from the Big 10, every major senior player in the league. While I was getting upset, Al seemed to enjoy the thought that he was almost assured of a victory. He was going to enjoy really putting the squeeze on me. But then Dick Enberg, Al, and I talked it over and decided it just made no sense for the three of us to be involved in an All-Star game when it had no real chance of success.

So we came up with a solution. We would have a draft of the available players. It wouldn't be the ACC against the Big 10, but it would be a balanced game. Dick would explain to the fans, who had bought tickets on the idea of a conference matchup, that the draft was held to keep the game competitive.

The next morning, Al and I got a wake-up call from the game committee. (When we're on the road together, we usually stay in the same room, since Al never sleeps in a bed anyway. When we have only one bed in the room, he lies on the floor and just curls up in his clothes. So he's never any trouble to be around.) The committee wanted to have a meeting downstairs to discuss the draft situation. Al said he wasn't going to any more meetings, and when Al says forget it, you forget it. I went downstairs myself and found Bobby Knight in the hallway. Bobby had had a terrible case of the runs caused by eating too much Mexican food at the Final Four in Albuquerque. He was kind of getting a kick out of the fact that I was in a tight squeeze because I had no ACC players to form a team, so I dragged him to this meeting with me.

At the meeting, I was informed the committee wasn't going along with the draft of the players. They still wanted to try to organize an ACC squad. At that point, they had five ACC players, none of whom had been a full-time starter or earned all-conference honors as a senior. So I had a very weak team and no substitutes. Bobby was sitting over in the corner, enjoying all of this. They explained that my team would be filled out with other people. They were flying in Dale Solomon. Solomon was good, but he played for Virginia Tech, which wasn't in the Atlantic Coast Converence. I said, if they were getting players outside the ACC, the game was no longer a Big 10–ACC matchup.

"You might just as well go ahead and really get some topflight players," I said, "kids who would be available from Louisville and other schools around the country, Kentucky and other Southeastern Conference teams."

"You're getting Dale Solomon," one committee member said. "You shouldn't complain. He's a great player."

Well, that comment stirred the wrath of Bobby Knight. Bobby had just coached the East-West All-Star Game in Albuquerque, and Dale Solomon was one of the players on his team. Bobby stood up and said, "He's not a great player."

"Oh, yes, he *is* a great player," the committee member told Bobby. The more the man was sure Solomon was a great player, the more Bobby questioned whether that man had the right to tell him who could play, particularly since Bobby had just coached Solomon a few days before. The next thing I knew, Bobby was chest to chest with the gentleman, telling him he didn't know who the hell could play and he had better leave basketball up to him.

"Packer and McGuire and Enberg were right," Knight said. "You'd better divide this team up or you're going to have a disaster."

People in Big 10 country know when Bobby Knight means business, so the committee decided the best thing to do was divide up the teams and play the game. Somehow, it turned out to be a great night of basketball. Bobby even divided the teams fairly. Al's team pulled it out at the end and I can still see Al walking across the floor with his hands in the air, victorious. I had suffered my first defeat in our All-Star challenges.

The people running the show in Cedar Rapids were not only very nice but also very naïve. A committee member mentioned that they had told the players to go over to a local sporting goods store and pick out some things that they might need.

Al jumped up, screaming, "That's the craziest thing I've ever heard of. Those kids are going to go crazy. They're going to run up a bill that you're not going to believe." You'd have thought they were spending Al's money.

The fellow said maybe it wouldn't be a problem.

Al said, "You guys are crazy. Those kids are going to tear you up over there at that sporting goods store."

It wasn't more than 20 minutes later that the guy came back to our room and said, "Oh, Al, we've got a serious problem. The bill is over $13,000."

Of course, Al got even more upset, although I thought it was kind of funny that the guys could have had enough ingenuity to spend $13,000 in that short a time.

We found out that the sporting goods store had opened the doors to them. When the kids were told to pick out what they wanted, they selected all kinds of warm-up uniforms to send home to friends. Fortunately, the owner of the store realized the circumstances and allowed the committee to return the merchandise.

We kept up the All-Star competition for a couple of years. In fact, we started an All-Star game with Dave Gavitt, the Big East commissioner, in Syracuse. That game could have been a total disaster on at least one occasion, but it was salvaged by the athletes. Many people have low opinions of college athletes, but the vast majority of kids playing ball today are very classy, except when they're turned loose in a sporting goods store in Cedar Rapids. Otherwise, they made our All-Star experiences a pleasure with the effort and work they put into performing. They were all responsible for their actions on and off the court. I think they're a real credit to their coaches and parents.

To the contrary, there was Al. You just never know what that man will do. I was meeting him in Syracuse, and my flight didn't get in until about 3:30 A.M. I quietly opened the door to our hotel room but found the light on and Al sitting up in bed.

"I can't sleep," he said. "I've really messed up. I went to the practice and didn't know who the players were." Of course Al wouldn't know one player from another because he doesn't follow the game that closely. But two players had been working out when he got to practice. One was from Connecticut and another from Providence. Both were small, and Al actually thought they were just school kids working out in the gymnasium. When the reporters asked him where the rest of the team was, Al said none of our players had shown up yet.

"But aren't the two guys out there playing for you?" the reporters asked.

"You've got to be kidding," Al said. "Those are just a couple of gym rats. They're not going to be playing for anybody."

Then the reporters informed Al who the two players were. At that point, Al went on the offensive and blamed things on Dave Gavitt, who is a good friend of ours, a guy we consider the top businessman in all of college basketball. Al criticized Dave and the Big East Conference for not doing the job and not getting the players there. He said we were doing all the work and nobody else was doing anything. Al just went off on a tangent. When he finished, he realized he had made a big mistake. He went back to his room just distraught. He didn't know what we were going to do. By the time I arrived at 3:30, I was able to see the guest list and confirmed that all the players had checked in. We had probably the finest collection of All-Star talent that would be on any one floor after the 1983–84 season. We had every major senior player there. Right down to the last man, Dave Gavitt had delivered every key senior player in the Big East with the exception of Gene Smith from Georgetown. Smith couldn't be there because

Georgetown's team banquet was on the same night as the game.

When I told Al about the players, he sighed with both relief and despair. "Oh, great," he said. "I didn't know what was going to happen. What we've got to do is beat the newspaper."

I said, "What do you mean, beat the newspaper?"

He said, "Well, the newspaper's going to come out and say our game is a disaster and nobody's showing up to play. We're going to have to get on all the phones and call all the radio stations. We'll get on the radio stations this morning and tell them about all the great players who are here."

That's exactly what we did. We got the word out that Sam Perkins had arrived, and Lancaster Gordon and Charles Jones from Louisville would be playing. We called the stations and went down the roster, identifying all the outstanding players we had there. We had pulled it off, turning a bad situation into a good one. It was probably the only time Al McGuire has been upset with the way he handled the press. Usually he is a real magician at it.

Al's snafu rivaled the big mix-up from the game's first year. Miller Beer was one of our corporate sponsors for the game, and we had given them the green light to do whatever they needed to promote Miller Beer. They went all out with banners and posters and did a terrific job. Al just loved it because he's a big promotion man anyway.

I got a call the afternoon of the game from Syracuse's athletic director, Jake Crouthamel. He said, "Billy, we've got a serious problem over here at the gymnasium. Today is freshman orientation day, and we're using the parking lot of the gymnasium for all the parents of the freshmen coming to Syracuse next fall." Then he said, "What are we going to do with the beer bottle?"

Beer bottle? I told him I really didn't know what he was talking about. He said, "You better get over here right away."

Well, it seems that Miller had attached one of those huge inflatable bottles right to the gymnasium roof. Obviously, it wasn't the best thing for parents to see as they drove into the parking lot for freshman orientation. But there was this giant beer bottle flying a hundred feet above the gym roof.

Al thought it was great and made sure that we had pictures taken of it before it was taken down. He wanted to take the photos back to the Miller Beer people to show them the tremendous exposure the All-Star game gave their product. It was a very embarrassing situation for Syracuse University, but for Packer and McGuire it was another promotion coup.

Al and I also dabbled a bit in tournament promotion with our friend, Dan Davis, the owner/operator of a Wendy's franchise in Bowling Green, Kentucky. Dan decided he wanted to put together a tournament, so Al and I arranged it for him. We brought in three outside teams to play against Western Kentucky as part of the Wendy's classic.

The weekend of the tournament, Al and I both had to broadcast games and then fly back to Kentucky for the Wendy's event. We decided that the executives from Wendy's and I would pick up Al in the company plane and then fly together to the tournament. I told Al to make sure he'd be ready to go Saturday when we flew into South Bend to pick him up. I told him to stay in his NBC attire, not to get into his "soft clothes," as he calls his vagrant outfits. I didn't want to have to track him down at the airport near the Space Invaders game, which was a big thing for Al at the time. He was one of the leading Space Invaders players in the United States. "All the corporate heads of Wendy's will be there," I told him, "so let's make a good impression."

When I went to meet the Wendy's people at the airport, I learned that they had decided not to go after all. It was just me and the Wendy's driver who had given me a lift to the airport.

I thought, "Oh, boy, I've got Al all fired up for nothing."

Then the driver said, "But I'd like to go. I've never flown on a corporate jet, and I love basketball. Since the plane's coming back after the game anyway, would you mind if I rode along?"

"Not at all," I said, and off we went to South Bend. As we

rode, I couldn't help thinking, "What a great setup for Al. He's going to think this fella riding with me is the president of Wendy's, and I'm never going to tell him otherwise."

We landed in South Bend, and there was Al standing at the end of the runway. He even had his NBC patch on his blazer. He was in such rare form. He jumped on the plane, smiling and very cordial. He shook the driver's hand.

I was laughing so hard to myself because Al had fallen for the trap. He thought this guy was the president of Wendy's and had taken the attitude "Billy, move aside because I'm really going to put the sales pitch on him." So I pretended I was asleep.

Al started talking about all the promotional things that could be done and how he and I could really set things up for Wendy's. "We'll do a job like you've never seen before," he said and went on and on and on. I wondered when he was ever going to let up. He wouldn't let the guy interject anything. Finally, the fellow said, "I think we've got some drinks and snacks on the plane. Would you like some?"

As he moved to the front of the plane, I opened up my eyes after pretending to be taking a cat nap, and said, "Al, let me tell you something."

He said, "Don't bother me, meathead. I'm on a roll."

I told him, "The fella's not the president of Wendy's. As a matter of fact, I don't even think he's the vice-president. As a matter of fact, I think he's only the guy in charge of driving me back and forth to the airport.

Al realized he had wasted one of his greatest sales pitches on a guy who was only our driver. He looked kind of blank for a minute and then hollered up to the guy, "Hey, I want a real stiff drink here. And Bill and I have a lot of talking to do. So how about you staying up there in the front and letting us sit back here and relax?"

I guess some rivalries go on forever. I'll probably never stop trying to get the best of Al, although I love the guy, and I *know* he'll never stop tormenting me. There's another rivalry, however, that goes back even further for me.

Lefty Driesell has been one of the great stories, as character and coach, in the history of collegiate basketball. My time with him goes way back to his very first game as a college coach, when he began his successful tenure at Davidson. The first victory that Lefty put on his coaching scoreboard was against the Wake Forest team I played for. It was very humiliating for Coach Bones McKinney and our team because Davidson College's program wasn't in very good shape when Lefty took over. Although we had a number of players injured to start the season, Wake Forest had a sound program. We had high aspirations and eventually realized them, winning the school's first two ACC championships and later making it to the Final Four. All the more reason for making this defeat at the hands of lowly Davidson a memorable game. Unpleasantly memorable, I should add. I was so humiliated that the next day I didn't go to classes. I didn't want to face students on the campus.

The next year, when Lefty brought his team back, we had a chance for revenge. Although normally we wouldn't have been so concerned about beating Davidson, our whole team looked forward to getting back at this fellow Driesell. We gave Lefty's team a pretty good whipping that night. When the game was over, we had that kind of puffy victory feeling. We had shown this upstart where he stood in basketball. I remember the reporters asking Lefty, "What do you think of Wake Forest now?"

He shot back, "Well, the way I look at it, guys, is that I'm one and one against Wake." I always admired that statement. He was looking ahead to the great program he was building at Davidson, a program such as the school had never seen, and he wasn't looking back at the mediocrity he had inherited.

It wasn't long before the tables were turned. Lefty built Davidson into a nationally ranked team. And I became an assistant coach at Wake Forest, first under Bones and then under Jack Murdock, and eventually under Jack McCloskey. In 1966, we weren't having a good year at Wake, but Lefty was enjoying the great program he had built. The teams met in the Greensboro Coliseum. Jack Murdock was in our locker room, preparing for the game. I thought we didn't have much of a chance against Davidson. While Murdock was talking to the team, I went to the bathroom, and while I was back there I realized I could hear Lefty talking to his players through the pipes. So our team gathered in the john to listen to Lefty. He was kind of putting our club down a little bit, and that fired our team up. We went out in the first half and played probably the best half of basketball we had played all year.

So I thought it was a good idea in the second half for us to go back into the bathroom and listen to what Lefty told his troops during halftime. Maybe that would keep our kids on a high. Lefty spent maybe the first 12 minutes of the halftime getting all over his ball players, just telling them how bad they were playing and how bad Wake Forest was, how this shouldn't even be a contest. Our kids were getting fired up as they sat and listened to the left-hander. He ended the speech by setting up a jump ball play to open the second half. We knew exactly what he was going to run, so we intercepted the ball, got our guys on a good start, and, lo and behold, upset Lefty's team.

If the left-hander had known what was going on, he might have realized he is now one and two against teams I've been affiliated with. If Lefty will ever take the time to read this book—and maybe I'll send him one because he might be too tight to buy one—he'll finally find out how we beat him in Greensboro that night.

CHAPTER

9

BONES

I came to the Atlantic Coast Conference in 1958, just as it was growing out of its infancy. The league, in those days, was colorful to the point of being outrageous. And nothing made it more so than Bones McKinney.

I accepted a scholarship at Wake Forest University with the idea I would be playing for a major college program in a major league. The ACC had just been formed in 1953, but within three short years, North Carolina had won its first NCAA Championship and C. D. Chesley had begun televising games. I just assumed everything at Wake Forest was going to be first class. I soon realized how wrong I was.

On the season's first road trip, the freshman and varsity teams traveled together on the bus down to Davidson College. We played well and won both games. I figured that afterward, we'd all go out and celebrate with a steak dinner before returning to Winston-Salem. But Bones just didn't work that way. We got back on the bus, rode down the road a little ways, and stopped at one of those grocery store–gas station combinations, the kind you see throughout the South. Bones got everybody off the bus and told us to go inside and pick out whatever we wanted, Nabs, potato chips, that kind of stuff. As I explained earlier, Bones was a great Pepsi drinker. For drinks, he got cartons of Pepsi and put them on the bus. There we were, having our post-game meal in first-class fashion after coming away with two victories.

We headed down the road, munching Nabs and drinking Pepsi, which was Bones's regular diet. I doubt if he ever ate any solid foods. For me, it was quite a letdown.

We'd traveled maybe 30 to 40 miles of our hour-and-a-half drive back, when Bones stopped the bus and announced that anybody who wanted to take a leak had better do it then. It was the last stop he was making before we got home. The veteran players on the team were used to that. Bones, his assistant coaches, and the players who had to, got off the bus in the middle of nowhere and took a leak along the side of the highway.

"Can you believe this?" I thought to myself. That trip was just my first lesson in the eccentricities of Bones McKinney. I would see quite a few of them over the next four years.

In those days, the Dixie Classic, a holiday tournament held in Raleigh, North Carolina, had quickly become a premiere event in college basketball. Like the ACC tournament, the Dixie Classic was a trademark of Southern basketball. The great enthusiasm today for basketball in North Carolina has much of its roots in the Classic. It was the place to be for the start of the season down South.

My first Dixie Classic opened the 1959–60 season, my sophomore year, which, in those days, was the first year of a player's eligibility for varsity ball. Wake Forest had an outstanding tournament that year and won its first trophy by beating North Carolina. Our program at Wake was on the rise, with players like Dave Budd, George Ritchie, and Len Chappell. The older players on the team had never enjoyed a winning record during their careers, but we were on the verge of changing that. Our championship continued a tradition of no team outside the ACC ever winning the Classic. And the outside competition wasn't weak. It included great clubs such as the University of Cincinnati team with Oscar Robinson and the Michigan State team with Johnny Green. Wake was able to knock off two fine teams from outside the South, Dayton and Holy Cross with Jack "the Shot" Foley. Carolina, still strong with several players from the 1957 national championship team, made it to the finals that year against us. The most deadly thing about Carolina was its great coach, Frank McGuire. Certainly the Heels were as good that year as Ohio State, which would end the season as the top team in the country.

We weren't held in the esteem that Carolina was, but we were fired up to play McGuire's team that night. Then Bones McKinney stood up in the locker room to talk to us.

Now, Bones was always doing a lot of thinking, and he had decided we would hold the ball against Carolina. He told us if we got the opening tip, we weren't going to shoot the ball at all. You can imagine our dejection. We were all in the mood to go out and play heads-up ball, really take it to them. We thought we were as good as Carolina, which may not have been the case. But the important thing was that we *thought* we were. The idea of playing stall ball was a real downer for all of us.

Bones was excellent at reading his team's emotions. He saw how we felt. But he had worked on the Carolina game plan for quite some time, and he really believed it would work. Bones decided he needed to sell the idea to us a little better.

"Fellas," he said, "we're only going to do this for a half, and I'll tell you why. The University of North Carolina has more depth than we have. They can afford to go ahead and get down into their other players.

"They have a reputation for winning games, so I think they have the referees in their favor. This is the kind of game that we may run into foul trouble early, so we're going to play them a half a game. I think we're a better team than they are, as long as we can keep our best people on the floor. For the second half, we'll go out there and show them that we can play right with them. We'll play our best five against their five."

Bones's game plan aggravated Frank McGuire a great deal, because we did get the opening tip and held the ball. The score at half time was something like 8 to 6. We went into the locker room feeling pretty good. But you can imagine where that left the University of North Carolina players. They had planned to come out and show their·basketball wares, and this team from Wake Forest was holding the ball.

I would have loved to have been a fly on the wall in Frank McGuire's locker room. Frank was a very proud man and a guy that always felt his team would win. Here he was in a championship that would add to the stature, the legend, of Frank McGuire, and could improve the ranking of University of North Carolina. And here was Bones McKinney and Wake Forest. Holding the ball. Killing a great game.

Over on our end of the floor, our thinking had changed. We felt Bones was nothing short of a genius. He had disappointed us before the game, but after a half of watching his theory work, we were ready to go out and win that second half. We had kept the score close without getting into foul trouble. What's more, we had conserved our energy. Stall ball doesn't require that much. By the second half tip off, we were primed for the upset.

When we came out charging in the second half, our sudden aggressiveness caught North Carolina off balance. Bones's game plan worked down to the tee. We came away with a very sweet victory that night, Wake Forest's first and only win in the Dixie Classic and certainly one of the highlights in my playing career and Bones McKinney's coaching career. I was named MVP of the tournament, the only sophomore ever accorded that honor.

It seemed to be a great start to the season. Bones, however, soon learned the stall-ball lesson. Dayton was one of the teams we had beaten in the tournament. The Flyers were a fine club, with a strong basketball tradition and a Top 10 ranking that year. Our win over them was another big moment for us, because it put Wake Forest into the position to be recognized nationally. Unfortunately, we had to play Dayton again, in Dayton, just a week after the Dixie Classic. And Bones was worried. It seems that the year before, the varsity won only eight games, but one of those victories had been against Dayton on Wake's turf. We had scored a ridiculously low number of field goals, something like six or seven, but still won the game because the referees constantly sent Wake to the foul line. And now Bones felt sure we would get a good dose of "home cooking" in Dayton, that the referees might favor them the way we had been favored before.

We arrived in Dayton looking forward to a rematch. So were the people in Ohio. I believe it was one of the state's first televised basketball games. The field house was jammed with people anticipating a little revenge for Dayton's two previous losses, the year before and then in the Dixie Classic.

"Look, fellas," Bones said in the locker room, "I know we're going to be in for a rough night tonight. The referees are going to remember last year's game down in Winston-Salem, and we're sure to get in foul trouble.

"So what we're going to do is the same thing we did against North Carolina ten days ago. We're going to hold the ball through the first half and only play them half a game. Since Dayton is a zone team, the score should be 0–0 at the half. If we get the opening tip, we're going to force Dayton to come out of that zone, or I'm going to force the referees to start this game with a technical foul."

Since the strategy had worked so well against Carolina, we were gung ho to try anything Bones had in mind. We won the opening tip. Dave Budd, our star forward, got the ball as he was instructed and stood at half court. The Flyers dropped back into their zone, and Bones started taunting the officials. I stood with my backcourt running partner, George Ritchie, off the side out near mid court. We just stood there and talked, while the fans began to show their annoyance. They started throwing things on the floor, chanting, and raising hell. The more they chanted, the more Bones fussed at the officials, calling them gutless for not assessing Dayton a foul for failing to come out of the zone to force the action.

The rules required that, but much to my surprise, the referees didn't call a technical foul. By the rules, Bones was right. The officials had good reputations, but that night they would not call the technical against Dayton. So Dave Budd merely stood there and held the ball.

George Ritchie and I had absolutely nothing to do, with the minutes going by and the score at zero. So we decided to call a play and just run the pattern to stay loose a little bit. We just ran through the traffic and came back out to the mid-court area. We hollered out a number and both of us took off and ran to the inside and came back out to center court, just something to amuse us and keep us moving. That confused Lenny Chappell, our All-American. He didn't remember us having a play by that number, and Bones hadn't mentioned anything about it in the game plan. So when I ran inside again, he asked me, "What in the world are you guys doing?"

"We're just making up plays and calling them," I said.

"Let me call one," he said. So during the rest of the half, Lenny occasionally would call out a play and smile, as if we were just ready to spring into action, which we had no intention of doing.

The minutes dragged by without a score. You can imagine how the fans felt about Bones McKinney and his strategy. You could feel the tension building. Later that night, a near riot erupted. It was probably fortunate for all of us that when we did begin playing, Dayton beat us thoroughly.

The abuse and trash directed at the bench was so strong that Bones feared somebody would get hurt. So with about six minutes left in the game, after we had dropped our strategy and Dayton had run away with the lead, he cleared out all the substitutes, telling the guys who weren't in the game to go shower so that we could get out of there. For those of us still playing, we had to put up with the abuse. Through it all, we could see our national ranking going down the drain because we were getting drubbed. And we were really annoyed with our coach. We wondered what we could have done to Dayton if we had just played a regular game.

And then the absolutely craziest thing happened. We had a player foul out of the game leaving us with only four players on the court. Bones said he wouldn't put in another player until he had used up the full sixty seconds allowed by the rules to make a substitution. Of course, there was nobody to put in because our bench had been cleared minutes before. Our subs were in the locker room taking a shower. So Bones asked the scorer's table to let him know when 59 seconds had passed so that he could call a time out. The scorer didn't notify him, and the ref called a technical foul against us for not having a substitute in the game in 60 seconds. That started Bones on another tirade with the officials. It was quite a show.

We, the Wake players, were almost openly rooting for the officials to throw Bones out of the game. Fortunately, one of our assistant coaches went into the locker room and pulled Twig Wiggins out of the shower to come back out and play. He was soaking wet, and, if I recall clearly, he didn't even have socks on.

You would assume that the Dayton fans would be very happy with their team's 17-point victory. The Flyers had reestablished themselves in the polls and knocked this up-start Wake Forest completely out of the national picture. But while we dressed in the locker room, we could hear this crowd of people storming outside, wanting Bones McKinney. They didn't want to honor him; they wanted to tear him apart. It was a terrible scene. Bones got us together in the locker room and said, "I know they want you guys, but we'll get out of here somehow. The police will handle this and get us out of the arena. Don't worry about a thing. Everything will be okay." Well, I don't know who it was but somebody said, "Coach, it doesn't sound like they want us. It sounds like they want you." The chants outside were, "We want Bones! We want Bones!"

Somehow we did get out of Dayton that night. It took a state police escort to get us on the bus. We all had to crouch on the floor because the people were throwing rocks and stuff at our windows. Talk about leaving with your tail tucked between your legs. It was a rather inauspicious journey back home.

If the University of North Carolina was the challenge of the ACC, the University of Virginia in those days was the breather. Playing against the Wahoos always seemed to produce some anecdote or story. The Virginia athletic program wasn't in good shape, with the football and basketball teams struggling.

Unfortunately, we always seemed to relax too much against Virginia. We would get behind but somehow we'd eventually pull out a win. It always seemed to come down to a serious scare. The Wahoos had one outstanding player, Paul Adkins, but not much else to go with him. With our attitude, it wasn't long before they had us in a real dog fight. It was my first varsity game against Virginia, and with about thirty seconds to go, we had a one-point lead, but they had the ball. Adkins had played well that night, and we were worried that we couldn't keep him from getting off a final shot.

We had everything to lose and nothing much to gain. Being beaten by Virginia would really dampen our effort to win the conference championship, which Wake Forest had never won. Virginia called a time out, and when we went to the bench, Bones was ready with a tongue lashing. How could we get ourselves in that fix? he asked. He tried to set up a defense to handle Adkins.

But when we walked back out on the court I noticed that Virginia had substituted a guy about 6'5" with a patch over his right eye at forward. I thought, "Boy, that's unusual. They put a guy in the game who's got a patch over his eye. I can shade away from that side of the floor because they're definitely not going to pass the ball to him." I figured maybe he was an outstanding leaper or rebounder put in there to get the ball if Adkins missed. Adkins was being guarded by George Ritchie, so I thought I'd shade over and help out with Adkins. Virginia worked the ball down into the right corner to the fellow with the patch over his eye. All of a sudden he decided to wheel to the basket and shoot a lefthanded hook shot. Obviously a lefthanded hook shot from a guy who has a patch over his right eye meant he didn't even see the basket. But he took the hook shot, and the ball went out of bounds, without hitting the rim, net, backboard, or anything. A complete air ball. We had the ball, and off we went down to the other end of the court to seal up the win. I remembered showering that night and wondering why in the world the Virginia people would put a guy in the game with a patch over his eye to take a last-second shot. I still don't have an answer, 25 years later, except that maybe they were hoping an absurd move would give them a lucky break and an upset victory.

The next year, when we played Virginia again in Charlottesville, Bones decided to have some fun with their coach, Bill McCann. Seeking to lend some drama to their program, Virginia would cut out the lights before the game and introduce their players with a spotlight. Bones decided to start all the big players on the team that night with the idea that they would be very impressive in the spotlight. Bones ran five players out there with incredible bulk, led by Lenny Chappell at 6'8", 240 pounds. The first Virginia player introduced was John Hasbrouck, who was 5'11" and 145 pounds. As Hasbrouck ran out, Bones yelled over to McCann, "I'll not play this game until that boy has a blood transfusion."

The crowd roared. Bones and Bill McCann were having a great time. But it all made concentration for the players very difficult. Worst of all, Bones's comments had fired up Hasbrouck, who was the man I was guarding. Not that I was a great defensive player or anything. But Hasbrouck played the game of his life that night, scoring 20 points or so. The last thing I had needed was my own coach getting him fired up.

But playing Virginia always seemed to bring out the unusual in Bones. One year we played the Wahoos in Charlottesville before Christmas. Our captain was Jerry Steele, who had had a very serious knee injury. But he had so much pride and the will to play with pain that he came back on the team just weeks after having a knee operation. For Jerry to compete, the team support people had to shoot up his knee to numb it. The game at Virginia was one of his first back, and he was still in a great deal of pain. But Bones felt we could beat Virginia without Jerry. So he kept him on the bench. Unfortunately, we were playing a very poor game that night and midway through the first half Bones said, "Jerry, I want you to go back in that wrestling room (Virginia had a wrestling room behind the main gym), and start running and warm that leg up. I'll call you when I need you."

Jerry was one of those people who would do anything for the team. I mean anything. So Jerry went back there with a swollen knee and a great deal of pain and started to loosen up. He ran and he ran through the remainder of the first half, and he jogged through halftime and through the second half. Near the end of the game, a concessions man happened to walk back there, and asked, "What are you doing?"

Jerry said, "I'm getting loose. Coach may be calling on me."

"I don't know why he'd be calling on you now," the man said. "Your team's ahead by 15 or 20 points. The game's getting ready to end."

Well, the game ended and Bones had forgotten all about Jerry. We went to the locker room and took our showers and everything. As we were counting up heads getting ready to go back on the bus somebody realized we were missing Jerry Steele. Bones sent a manager out for Jerry, and there he was, still loosening up back in the wrestling room because he hadn't had the order from Coach McKinney that the game was over.

That night, there had been an incredible snowstorm. Bones said we might as well stay in Charlottesville and try to reach Maryland for our next game in the morning. But I was worried we'd get stuck in Charlottesville, so I said to Bones, "We're all kind of keyed up from playing the game. We're going to have to play tomorrow afternoon. Why don't we just go ahead and take the bus ride? We'll sleep on the bus just as well as we'd sleep in the room."

We looked at each other and Bones said, "Well, that sounds

like a decent idea to me. Let's go ahead." We got the bus driver and off we went to the University of Maryland. The weather was a lot worse than we had anticipated. We didn't get to D.C. until about three-thirty in the morning. Upon arriving in the city limits, the bus driver said, "Look, I'm out of gas. I have to go to the Greyhound terminal to fill up. I'd hate for us to get stuck in the snowstorm."

We pulled up into the Greyhound bus terminal where he gassed up. Here it was the middle of the night, we were all hungry and tired and sleeping on the bus hadn't been as easy as I thought it would be. Bones was looking at me kind of cross-eyed by that time. We waited for the bus to fill up, and an hour later we were ready to go again. Unfortunately for us and the bus driver—because he never heard the last of this from Bones McKinney—our hotel turned out to be two blocks from the terminal. We could have walked down there and gotten in bed. Bones told our trainer, "Let them sleep for an hour or so. Then I want everybody up at seven and taped and ready to go to the game. If they start sleeping too long their heads are going to get soggy. Just go ahead and tape them up at seven-thirty." I suppose the strangest thing of all was that we had an outstanding game against the University of Maryland.

I recall the first time the team traveled to D.C. I was eager to go there because I had never been before. And for me, and most ball players, travel was part of the excitement of participating. As for my first trip to Washington, I thought we'd be staying in a plush hotel and doing some sightseeing. When we got there, we pulled up to a place called the Dobbs House. It didn't look too good. We walked inside and found a number of elderly people sitting around. The place was in shambles, and Bones says "Everybody check in."

To give you an idea of how antiquated this place was, there were no TVs in the rooms, just radios. And they were old-time radios, where you had to put a quarter in the back slot in order to get it to play. The beds were sagging; the mattresses were almost down to the floor. Our bigger players couldn't even sleep there. Of course, we were all upset with

Bones. Being a spokesman, I had to go down to his room and say, "Coach, what in the world are we doing staying in a hotel like this, in a town that obviously has outstanding accommodations?"

Obviously, a player shouldn't say things like that to a coach, but then again there wouldn't be many coaches today who would go to Washington, D.C., and stay in a place like that, which, we found out, had been changed from a hotel to a home for the aged. Well, Bones said it was none of my business and that that was where we were going to stay. He told me to go back up to my room and get myself mentally prepared for the game. But my inquisitive nature had been stirred. I had to check out just exactly what the story was. To find out, I went to Skeeter Francis, who was then our sports information director and is now an administrator with the ACC main office. He told me that the Dobbs House had once been an outstanding hotel in Washington, D.C. It had been the home of the old Washington Capitals of the NBA. That's where Bones stayed when he was a professional playing for Red Auerbach and the Washington Capitals. In those days, the Capitals held the record for the most consecutive wins, something like 17 or 18. During that winning streak Bones McKinney and his teammates stayed at the Dobbs House. So Bones, a superstitious creature with his red socks and Pepsi Colas and packs of Nabs, fell back on what had worked before. He decided that if the Capitals had maintained a winning streak staying at the Dobbs House, it would be best for Wake Forest to start a streak by staying there. It didn't quite work that way, however. The next night we played against George Washington University and lost in one of our poorest performances of the year. The luck of the Dobbs House had run out.

Of my time at Wake Forest, I treasure most my associations with my teammates and coaches and the people I competed against. Of all those memories, perhaps the finest game I ever participated in was our 1961 match-up against St. Bonaventure in the East Regional semifinals in Charlotte,

North Carolina. The Bonnies had an outstanding team, one of the premiere clubs in the country that year, headed by their All-American Tom Stith. We had just come off a victory over another of the country's finest teams, St. John's, in Madison Square Garden. Both St. John's and Bonaventure were Top Five caliber teams, right behind the top clubs of Ohio State and Cincinnati.

We knew we were going to have problems against Bonaventure in that we couldn't stop Stith. He was too quick and had too many moves around the basket. Nobody in the country could stop him one-on-one, not even our All-American center, Len Chappell. So Bones decided to play another one of our big men, Bill Hull, against Stith. Hull was a great athlete, with tremendous speed. He was 6'6" and weighed about 235 pounds. He was a Wake Forest football player who Bones had recruited to help fill a void caused by injuries at the start of the season. Bill had great leaping ability and upper-body strength. Bones thought that if Hull could stay with Stith as long as possible, we might just have a chance to knock off Bonaventure.

The game proved to be everything the fans wanted, one of those seesawing contests with the lead switching by the minute. Nobody seemed capable of getting more than a one-point margin. It remained that way up to the halfway point of the second half, about ten minutes left. By then, Bill Hull had played himself to near exhaustion and needed to sit down for a while. Bones was faced with a real decision. He had to substitute with someone who could hold down Stith's scoring through this important stretch of the second half. He decided to go with 6'11" Bob Woollard, who was normally our starting center. Sometimes Bob played well and sometimes he didn't. We had to assume that with Stith's quickness, Bob would have his hands full. Bones told everyone playing in the game to sit down and rest during the time out. Then he turned all of his attention to Bob. "Just take a look at Bill, how hard he's worked, how tired he is," Bones said. "Look at how much he's given to the ball club. Bob, we want you to go in there and give us about two or three minutes until Hull is rested. During that time, do the best you can to stay with Stith. Let's not mess this ball game up. We've worked too hard to let it get away from us."

In an interview with Smith Barrier, Bones recalled the game like this:

About five minutes in the second half, Hull hits his tummy. That means, coach, I'm tired, take me out. We were just down five points and I said, "Lord, what am I going to do? I can't play." I look down the bench . . . and way down at the end was Woollard. He's talking to the cheerleaders. He didn't know what he was going to do during the game but he knew what he was going to do afterward.

I went down there and knelt in prayer, mostly, in front of him, slapped him . . . and got his attention right away. Told him ol' Hull was tired, needed two or three minutes rest, just go in there and play two or three minutes like I know you can, deep in your heart, and gave him a slap and he knocked me on my tail when he charged by me to the scorer's table. But he forgot who he was going in for, so he came back, and I wrote it on a piece of paper for him.

The first time Stith shot it, Woollard blocked it and picked off the ball. He gave the outlet to Bill Packer. When Billy tells it on TV today, he says you ought to pass here or pass there, but when he played for me, he wouldn't give the ball to his mother. Billy makes it, we're down by three. In nine minutes, fifty-four seconds Woollard blocks four shots, gets eleven points and ten rebounds, and we went from five down to five up. That's what you call coaching.

I wasn't going to take him out. I knew he might die, but I thought dying for me was a good reason. So I called a timeout. You see Duke, Carolina, State, they all run to the huddle. Not with me. That's the worst odor I ever smelled. It's terrible. They're spitting on the coach, garlic, BO, everything else. Just five players and when I looked up, four had their heads turned, and Woollard was sucking what air was in there. What he wanted to know was, "Coach, how much time before two or three minutes are up?"

As Bones recalled, we were all a little apprehensive about what would happen when Stith got the ball and turned to face Woollard. We could see Stith giving those eight million moves and fakes headed to the basket. As soon as St. Bonnie got the ball, their guard punched it inside to Stith. He turned and faced Woollard, but Bob didn't go for any of his fakes. Stith seemed almost frustrated and decided to go ahead and put up that odd left-handed shot of his. Woollard smacked it right out of bounds. For the next five or six minutes, Bob Woollard played as fine a game of basketball as anybody in the country could play against a guy like Stith.

After several minutes had gone by, I was bringing the ball down the floor, when it occurred to me that Bones might be getting ready to send Hull back in the game. I looked over to the bench, which in those days was at the end of the court, not at the side. There sat the coach with his arms tight around Hull, squeezing him tight, making sure he never did get back in the game. Woollard was the guy who gave us the win that night.

There was one other little factor that I ought to clear up about that game. To this day, the people at St. Bonaventure still talk about that game and say that Bones made the winning pass from the bench. That really wasn't the case, but I have to admit that Bones did get into the action a little more than he was supposed to that night.

The Bonnies had lost the ball out of bounds near their basket. The ball bounced over to Bones, and he was a very active coach on the sidelines anyway. He scooped up the ball and prepared to play. I was out near mid court when I realized he had it. I stepped out of bounds because you had to handle the ball from the side in those days. Bones fired a pass to me on the sidelines, while Allie Hart was breaking for the basket. I hit Hart with the pass, and he laid it up. It wasn't a direct pass from Bones to Hart, as some later alleged. But it was another quick maneuver that the officials never caught. And it led to a basket. Since we won the game by only two points, I guess the St. Bonaventure people are right in claiming it was the winning basket.

The year after I graduated from Wake Forest, Bones pulled one of his greatest stunts of all time. His team was playing at the University of Kentucky in the Kentucky Invitational Tournament against Princeton and Bill Bradley. It was a night in which Bones made the most of his tremendous ability to stir up a crowd. He was in constant motion on the sideline. It boggles the mind to think what he would do with today's rule about the coaching box. At one point in his career, his assistants decided to restrain him with a seat belt, to keep him from bolting off the bench to lead cheers or argue with the refs. That night in Kentucky, he wasn't wearing a seat belt, but he probably needed one. There was a great play, and Bones kicked up his heels. He used to wear these loafers that would constantly flop on the back of his feet, and when he kicked up his heels that night, one loafer went flying onto the floor just as Wake Forest had headed down court in the other direction. Bones realized the shoe was on the floor and ran out to pick it up and put it back on his foot before the team returned to his end of the court. But when he bent over to pick up the shoe, pens and papers fell out of his pocket onto the court. Suddenly, Princeton made an interception and headed back down the court toward Bones. Rather than hurry out of the way, Bones looked up, saw the Princeton break coming and started to play defense. Unbelievably, the referees didn't call a technical foul on him. In fact, his little show didn't even interrupt the game in any way, shape, or form—if you can believe that. Then again, a lot of things Bones did were simply unbelievable.

He was a Baptist minister, and an excellent one, too. Next to Billy Graham—and I say this in all deference to Mr. Graham—Bones was probably as popular a minister as there was in the state of North Carolina. He was very much in demand and constantly on the move, not only as a coach but as a preacher. It was an odd combination, coach and preacher. I don't think that had been done anywhere before and if it had, not to the degree that Bones McKinney carried on. In fact, *Life* magazine did a complete piece on Bones:

Baptist Minister, Preacher, Basketball Coach at Wake Forest University. Bones was very proud of that article.

Still, it wasn't always easy to be a basketball player when your coach was a minister. Games and practices were highly competitive. We were putting together an excellent team, so there was a lot of competition for jobs. Attitudes and emotions sometimes ran high, evidenced by occasional vulgar language. Well, when you played for Bones McKinney, bad language was out of the question. If you ever used it in front of him, on the court or off, you'd find yourself heading for the locker room with a pretty stern lecture from him on how you'd better start shaping up.

Once, when we were sophomores, Bones was holding a practice during Thanksgiving. On that particular morning we went up on the court at about nine A.M., and Bones was really on a roll. Instead of the normal 30 to 45 minutes, we worked until about noon. And Bones was still talking.

Finally, Tommy Vaughan, our manager, decided to remind Bones that it was time for lunch. Now, I'm going to pause here to emphasize that despite being a preacher, Bones had a very storied past. He had been involved in the NBA in its early stages. He was a street-smart guy, and his conversion to a minister had shocked a lot of people, because he had been a real rounder in his days as a player. Although it shocked some of his acquaintances, his conversion to minister was complete. I had never heard anything off-color out of his mouth from the first time I met him when I was a high school player.

So when Tommy went over that morning to tell Coach that we were going to miss lunch, Bones just turned and looked at him. I guess he was deeply engrossed in his teaching that day and not thinking because he looked at Tommy and grabbed himself in the crotch and said, "Tommy, I've got your lunch right here."

We were all shocked. We didn't know what to say. Here was our coach, the minister, making a lewd joke. We didn't know how to respond. All of a sudden Bones started laughing, and then we all started laughing. It occurred to us that although coach was a minister, he'd had quite a past and it wasn't completely out of him. Maybe his ability to share an off-color joke every now and then increased the bond between players and coach. Whatever you can say about that incident, after that day our relationship with him wasn't quite so strict. And that seemed healthy for both sides.

Although those days at Wake Forest seemed a bit hectic, my love and affection for Bones have only increased over the years.

CHAPTER

10

ON THE ROAD

John Madden says he can't handle airplanes and flying, so he takes the train to each of his broadcasting assignments. I've taken only a couple of train trips, and I hope I don't have to take any more unless I want a leisurely trip into the mountains somewhere. How Madden gets by with a train's pace I'll never know. Basketball broadcasters could never meet their schedules working from trains. That's why we prefer the skyways.

I admit to taking secret pleasure in amazing people with my travel schedule. You may see me at a game one afternoon in one state, and later that very evening I'll be working a game on television in another part of the country. All of it hinges on my ability to hop around quickly on airplanes. And when the planes don't work, I have a knack for finding another way through the snowdrifts or hailstorms to a game.

Eddie Einhorn used to get a kick out of following my travels. In the mid-1970s, when Einhorn put together the original college basketball broadcast package for NBC, he had a few laughs watching me make the hectic schedule I had set up for myself. I was doing national games for NBC as well as the regional broadcasts for C. D. Chesley's ACC basketball network. I thought I had been pretty slick in arranging things that season, until one weekend near the end, when I found myself in quite a bind. I was working the ACC tournament for Chesley in Greensboro, North Carolina. Two games were scheduled Thursday afternoon and two more that night. Then there were two semifinal matches on Friday evening and the championship Saturday night. In a matter of three days, I was scheduled to work seven games for Chesley. Unfortunately, I had an NBC game to do in the middle of that. The network hadn't shown the University of San Francisco's undefeated team all season and was somewhat embarrassed, so Eddie Einhorn added San Francisco at Notre Dame that Saturday afternoon. The network also had me assigned to do a Sunday game, between Michigan and Marquette. I figured there would be plenty of time to make the Sunday game. But then Einhorn added the San Francisco game, and I was suddenly doing nine games in four days in three different cities.

There was no problem in chartering a private plane to take me from Greensboro to the University of Michigan after the Saturday night game. But the San Francisco game in Indiana really presented a hurdle. I thought about telling Chesley I couldn't do the ACC championship game Saturday night because I had the afternoon game in South Bend, but I didn't want to do that. Instead, I began putting together an airplane shuttle that would allow me to make all the games. Then I found out that propeller-driven planes couldn't get there quickly enough. I had to explore the possibility of renting a jet. The enormous expense was an immediate drawback. Even back in 1976, the cost was high, about $3,000.

The plane could hold six passengers. I started thinking about it and came up with the idea of a "Basketball Junkie's" weekend. I would take four friends with me, each of them putting up $700. For that, they would get air travel, hotel rooms, meals, and tickets to the nine games. The jet could easily make the trips, weather permitting. Finding four buddies was no problem. I put the weekend together without telling Chesley or the network people.

It was one of the all-time travel weekends. I worked the first six ACC games through Friday. Then the entourage and I jumped our jet for South Bend, a flight of an hour and 15 minutes. We got into our hotel rooms a little after 1:00 A.M. Saturday. That next morning I got up and pretended I'd been there for a good night's sleep. I went to the arena and watched Notre Dame knock off undefeated San Francisco (the Irish take pride in deflating championship seasons). It was a great day for the golden dome. Digger Phelps kept his players in the locker room until the very last moment to get them charged up. When they emerged, the crowd sent up a roar like I'd never heard before. The fans threw rolls of toilet paper on the floor, and the San Francisco players stopped their warm-up shooting to watch the celebration.

It was too much for the undefeated Dons. They lost their first game of the season and dropped from their number one ranking.

It was a great afternoon of basketball. And the ACC tournament had been tremendous. Then the four junkies and I had a police escort to our waiting jet. As we boarded the plane, the Southeastern Conference championship between Tennessee and Kentucky was just getting started. We arrived in Greensboro, where a car was waiting to take us to our hotel. There we had some dinner and watched the second half of the Tennessee-Kentucky game on a TV set in our little private dining area in the hotel restaurant.

A couple of basketball fans walked by, and one of them said, "Naw, that can't be Billy Packer. He just did the Notre Dame game I saw on TV this afternoon."

"I'm pretty sure that's who it is," the other one said.

"Naw," the guy said again. "No way. He's in Notre Dame."

That night, Jim Thacker and I broadcast the 1977 title game between Carolina and Virginia. Carolina won, and boom, we were back on the plane again, off to Ann Arbor for the Michigan-Marquette game. By that time, my fellow junkies were getting a little upset with me because some of my arrangements were less than the best. I did have the hotel rooms taken care of in Notre Dame, but the tickets that had been promised for the game weren't available. Instead, I had to get some private chairs and put my buddies right behind me in the broadcast area. That made for excellent seats but left them a little nervous about further ticket arrangements. But after eight games in three days, they were a little slaphappy. They started kidding me about forgetting to make room arrangements. I assured them I had. But then we rolled into Ann Arbor at about 1:00 A.M., and, sure enough, there weren't enough rooms for everybody. I had messed up. We had to bunk together, which meant more razzing for me.

Things got worse the next day. The tickets set aside in Michigan were as far away from the court as they could be. The guys really got on my case and said they were going to sit closer. Under pressure, I worked out a deal to get them some great seats, where they watched Michigan knock off Marquette.

When the game was over, we boarded our jet for Greensboro, ending four days of basketball madness from Greensboro to South Bend to Greensboro to Ann Arbor to Greensboro. Eddie Einhorn called me right after that weekend, laughing. "Someday you and I will have to do business together. Any guy who can pull off that schedule has to be somebody I can make some money with."

My ACC moonlighting got me in trouble again a few years later. Dick, Al, and I were doing a Sunday game, Maryland at Notre Dame, always a difficult place to reach in winter. On Saturday, I did an ACC game and then flew to Chicago, where I planned to pick up a small plane to South Bend. The hitch in my plans was that a severe snowstorm had hit Friday night. Indiana State Police put out emergency warnings and then sealed off the state. No traffic was allowed on the roads. And the South Bend airport was closed, nixing my flight plans. Al, having lived in Milwaukee, was prepared for the weather and made sure he got to Notre Dame early. But Dick Enberg was coming from California and wasn't any more prepared than I was.

I arrived in Chicago Saturday evening, and I was confident that I had time to make the game. I decided to get a rental car and drive down. I figured it would be no problem, a few hours and a little snow. When I went for the car, the rental clerks asked me where I was headed. I told them, and they informed me that Indiana State Police had told them not to rent cars to anyone going to Indiana. I was in a hell of a bind and figured I better call NBC.

The network people told me to rent a room, that they would work things out. Enberg had been in Chicago but somehow arranged to rent a car. He got as far as Gary, Indiana, before getting stuck. While he got a state trooper to bring him back to Chicago, I was supposed to find a private plane. After trying a while for a plane, I realized a helicopter would do the trick. So I scheduled one. I met Dick at about 1:00 A.M. and told him to get a good night's sleep because we would be leaving early in a helicopter.

"There's no way I'm going down in a helicopter," Dick said. "The hell with the game. It's not so important that I have to ride in a helicopter. They make me nervous. I'm not going."

I decided I'd better keep looking for a plane. At about 3:00 A.M., I found a pilot brave enough to fly his two-engine plane. We worked an agreement with the South Bend airport to clear away enough snow for us to land. We left at 8:00 that morning. It was absolutely beautiful, one of the most interesting flights I've ever taken. Indiana was a sight. There was so much snow, all you could see was white. The snow was up to the second stories of the houses, and the cars were entirely covered. The smokestacks and tops of tractor trailers were visible, but nothing else. I started thinking how pretty it was, until I realized there were people stranded in those trucks. I couldn't even see the cars. Our travel problems suddenly seemed small compared to those of the people trapped beneath us.

Then it came time to land. The snow on the runway was 6 feet deep with drifts up to 20 feet. The airport crew had cleared a landing area about the length of an aircraft carrier deck, or at least it seemed that way to me. We circled around, looking down and wondering if the plane had enough room. I've never landed on an aircraft carrier, but this had to be close to the real thing. Dick and I decided that, if the pilot was willing to try, so were we. He set it down with the plane coming to a stop about three yards from the end of the strip, right next to a packed snowbank.

We were left standing in these 6- to 10-foot snowbanks. Finally, a National Guard jeep picked us up and took us to the game. There was more snow than I'd ever seen. Notre Dame officials wanted a crowd for the game, so they offered free passes to anyone who would walk. Still, there were plenty of people in South Bend who thought good old-fashioned foot travel was too risky for that weather.

The next time I got tangled up in schedules, it was my travel agent's fault. Since then, I've taken to making more of my own arrangements. I've come to like working out tricky travel plans.

My agent appeared to have put together a decent schedule for me. I was doing a Sunday NBC game in Columbus, Ohio, between Ohio State and Virginia, and I had another game in Lexington on Monday night.

Monday, I went to the airport and asked a fellow where I could find Sky Train Airlines. My agent had given me a Sky Train ticket with the destination printed on it. The guy said he didn't know of any airline with that name. I went to the American Airlines counter for information and was told that Sky Train had gone out of business a couple of months earlier. "They don't even fly anymore," the clerk said.

I asked for an American flight to Lexington. The clerk said, "Fine. The next flight's tomorrow morning." There was no plane to Lexington that afternoon, and my game was only a few hours away. I started to panic. I figured the only way I could make the game was to get a rental car and drive as fast as I could to Lexington. I did that, but when I got out on the highway, I realized I had only had about two hours of sleep and was too tired to drive all that way alone. I thought, if I could get a hitchhiker to drive part of the way, I could get a half hour nap. That would leave me in good shape for the ball game.

It began snowing around Columbus. Finally, I saw two people hitchhiking. In a split instant, I decided to pick them up. I could get in the back seat and sleep while they drove. They were dressed in big parkas and hoods and stood by the road with the snow blowing all around them.

I quickly pulled over, got out, and cleaned my luggage out of the back seat. I had opened up the trunk and was putting in my luggage just as these two hooded people, a guy and a girl, walked up. They were going to Florida, which was in the same direction as Lexington. "That's perfect," I said. "I'm going to Lexington. I want you people to do the driving, and I'm going to sleep."

I jumped in the back seat, they got in the front, and off we went. I was asleep in no time. I can snooze at the drop of a hat when I'm traveling. I didn't stop to think these two people might be nervous about a guy who picks them up in a snowstorm and lets them do the driving, gets in the back seat and pretends like he's sleeping. When I woke up an hour or so later, we were just outside Cincinnati, heading south. I found out they had just decided that afternoon to go to Florida to get married. They got all their belongings, which amounted to a couple of suitcases, and took off to set up a new life for themselves. They had no money, no job, nothing. I said, "Hey, we're makin pretty good time here. Why don't you let me buy you something to eat?"

The girl turned around quickly and said, "Honestly, we're not trying to cause you any trouble. We'd never harm anybody."

"Why are you worried about that?" I asked.

She hesitated and then asked, "Do you have a gun on us?"

"What do you mean, a gun on you?" I said.

"Well," she said, "you're in the back seat, and we're scared to death that you're back there and you might try to do something strange."

I laughed and said, "No, no, I was just tired and needed to get an hour or so of rest." We stopped and ate, and then they really pushed it down the highway. When we got to Lexington, I dropped them off and headed to Rupp Arena. I was wearing khaki pants and an old beat-up shirt and needed to change. When I pulled up at the Hyatt near the arena, the scene was a typical Kentucky pregame celebration with a jazz band. The whole shebang. All the fans were fired up. My watch said a quarter to eight, and the tip-off was at eight. I had to change my clothes on the move, or I would miss the tip. I ran up to the bell captain, and he gave me a closet to change in. Then I hustled over to the arena, ran down the stairs, and saw my broadcast partner, Jay Randolph, standing at the end of the court, holding a microphone. I sidled up right beside Jay. He grabbed my shoulder and started off, "This is Jay Randolph from the Rupp Arena in Lexington, Kentucky, here for a great Southeastern Conference game between the University of Kentucky Wildcats and the LSU Tigers. Billy, what do you think of tonight's ball game?"

I panicked and realized my watch must have been off. We were on the air and I hadn't even had my mind set as to what we were doing. I answered Jay as well as I could. I was halfway through my answer when Jay said, "Nice job, Billy. Good rehearsal."

I was ready to kick him. If he'd only known what a rough time I'd had getting to the game, well, he'd never have believed it.

When NCAA tournament time comes each year, I have one goal: to see as many teams as possible as the field develops. That was a tough thing to do in the years before ESPN and the rise of the VCR unit. Now I can tape those shows I miss and see them later. But in the old days, the only way to do it was to hop around a lot, hustling to catch games here and there.

In the late seventies, I was assigned to opening-round games at Purdue University and Bowling Green, Kentucky. Purdue had a home-court advantage against St. John's, while the University of Kentucky, Florida State, Virginia Tech, and Western Kentucky were scheduled to play in Bowling

Green. I wasn't as familiar with those four teams as I wanted to be. So I decided to catch the game at Purdue on Thursday night and then fly down to Bowling Green to watch those games Friday with Dan Davis. Dan had agreed to send a plane up for me Friday, and NBC wouldn't even know I was gone. Afterward, I could get back on the plane and fly back to Purdue to announce the next round of games there on Saturday.

The plan was good for two reasons. It allowed me to learn more about the teams, and it cut out an absolutely boring day between games in Purdue, where I would have had to sit around doing nothing. At tournament time, I get pumped up to do as many games as I can. I like getting that overview, that understanding of how magnificent the tournament really is.

Things worked smoothly at first. I got to see the games Thursday night, and Dan's plane took me down to Bowling Green on Friday. We had a nice dinner and went to the games Friday night. Dan's favorite team is Western Kentucky, which unfortunately blew a big lead and lost to Virginia Tech. That left Dan very unhappy and set up the University of Kentucky for an easy march through the opening rounds.

When the games ended, Dan took me out to the airfield. Before I got on the plane, he said, "Hey, Bill, you ought to stay here for the night. It's about midnight. You could go up in the morning. That would be easier traveling."

"No," I said, "the people at NBC would be going through the ceiling now if they knew I wasn't in West Lafayette, Indiana. I'd better get up there."

Unfortunately, I wasn't aware the area just to the north had been going through some very rough weather. I got in the plane, a twin-engine job, and the pilot said, "You know, Mr. Packer, you'd better buckle up back there. We're going to run into some pretty severe thunder showers when we get up to the Indiana border."

I didn't think much about it. The night was nice and clear in Bowling Green. I strapped myself in, and, as usual before we left the runway, I was sound asleep. However, on this trip

I didn't sleep long. Before I realized it we were in broad daylight, or what seemed like broad daylight. The lightning was so severe that it lit up the whole sky and kept it lit. Just like noon with the sun shining. The thunder was banging. And the windshield was awash with water, like running your car through one of those automatic car washes. The noise and shaking had awakened me like an alarm clock. I was shocked at first. The plane was being rattled around, one of the most frightening rides I've ever been on.

It's the only time I've ever been on a plane when I really thought it was all over. I thought about my family, my insurance policies, what a great life it had been. Then abruptly the storm cleared about 10 miles out of West Lafayette, and we were able to land about 3 A.M. I was never so happy to put my feet on the ground. The propellers were still going when I got off the plane. I hollered to the pilot that he should stay with me and go back in the morning rather than fly back in that storm.

"No," he said, "I think I'll head back tonight."

I just stood there and watched in disbelief as he headed back down the runway and took off. I was thinking how foolish I was to make the trip just because of a game. Basketball junkies may be crazy, but the wildest sons of bitches in the world are private plane pilots.

I was once assigned to cover a 1978 opening-round NCAA tournament game between Indiana State and Virginia Tech in Lawrence, Kansas. Indiana State, with Larry Bird, was undefeated, but I hadn't done any of their games. I had made a remark in midseason that Indiana State didn't deserve to be number one, and the people from NBC were worried that the Indiana State people might be upset with me.

On my way to Lawrence to cover the game, I decided to stop in Chicago to meet with the people from McDonald's about their All-American game. Then I would go from Chicago to Lawrence.

That afternoon, I geared my schedule to leave Chicago,

catch a flight down to Wichita, and then take a smaller plane into Lawrence. Despite the precautions I had made to be on time, I got stuck on the Eisenhower Expressway and found traffic backed up to where it looked like I would miss my flight. It had been a relatively nice day in Chicago, so the cab driver and I assumed there must have been some kind of an accident on the expressway. The driver said the traffic wasn't normally that heavy, but he thought we would make the flight. We didn't realize it at the time, but tremendous tornado-type winds had blown through Chicago, taking a great deal of glass from buildings near O'Hare airport, knocking the roofs off some of the adjoining hotels, and generally creating havoc in the area. That had caused the traffic jam. When I got out to the airport, I learned all flights were late, but eventually I made it to Wichita, despite a rough flight through more tremendous winds from tornadoes.

In Wichita, my problems really began. I arrived at this little private air commuter terminal, where the pilot told me there were no more flights to Lawrence, but that he would go ahead and fly me over there for the same fare. We walked outside, and the wind was blowing pretty strongly. Without wasting time, we got on the plane, a basic six-seater with room for two pilots and four passengers. On this trip, however, there were only the two of us. I was kind of tired and fell asleep briefly. When I awakened and looked out the window, we were moving along at a low altitude but at a pretty good speed for a little plane like that. I mentioned to the pilot, "Seems like we're making pretty good time."

He said, "Oh, yeah, we've got a pretty good tail wind tonight. As a matter of fact, if you'll look down there, we're approaching Lawrence."

I looked down, and, sure enough, there was Lawrence. It sure seemed like a quick trip to me. As we started to come down and go around the field, I realized that the pilot was having an awful hard time landing the airplane. I wasn't too concerned immediately, but when we went down to hit the runway, we missed by a good hundred yards to the right. I leaned forward in my seat and said, "Gee, you having some trouble out there?"

He said, "No, not so much trouble. I think I'm going to circle again. I've got to allow for the crosswinds a little bit, but I don't think we'll have too much problem."

We started off again, and the second time we were still way to the right of the runway. We started in, but the plane was drifting severely to the left. Finally, we touched down in what was a daredevil landing, but the minute the plane hit the ground the wind just picked it right back up off the ground again and put us back in the air. The pilot finally brought it back down.

I thanked the pilot and asked whether the winds might have been too strong for the plane.

He said, "Oh, this plane can handle pretty strong winds."

Well, little did I know that these were 85-mile-per-hour winds, and we had just gone through a tornado. They were bending the trees over. When we went inside the trailer that served as a station, the man behind the desk started screaming at him, "You mean to tell me you flew in here? All planes have been grounded. How the hell did you get in here?"

The pilot said, "I just brought the plane in here."

The station manager said, "Those are tornado winds out there! That plane is not capable of flying." And he fired the pilot on the spot.

If I had known that we were in that kind of danger, my tail would have stayed in Wichita, and I would have gotten to the Indiana State game some other time.

If my travels gave me some harrowing experiences, they were nothing compared to what it was like traveling with Al McGuire.

Even though we didn't work for the same television networks, Al McGuire and I began doing radio shows in 1982 for Mutual Sports. Thinking we were both creative in recognizing and pursuing the good stories in basketball, I arranged for us to put together a daily radio show. Through the season, we run into an endless number of ideas, topics, people, information, etc. They all become the basis for stories about players or teams or games or just odd things going on in basketball. On the air, we fire opinions at each other in lively discussion.

Doing the show, working with Al, is very enjoyable, except for finding the time and making the arrangements to get together to tape the shows. We always seem to wind up in a mad hunt for a little peace and quiet to get our work done. Because we both crisscross the country covering games, the shows are usually produced under odd circumstances. At times, we've found ourselves recording shows in the most unusual places, the back seat of a taxicab or the men's room of Chicago's O'Hare International Airport. Seldom do we have the luxury of radio studios and top-rate technical equipment. In our rush, we're lucky to have a cassette recorder and a drugstore tape.

Our taping session in the rest room at O'Hare wasn't done by design, believe me. I had set up a meeting once with Al. He and I both happened to be flying into O'Hare, so it seemed like a good idea to meet in the Eastern Airlines lounge and record a few sessions. We got into Chicago on time, but when we got to the lounge, we realized the loud background noise would distort our shows. We had to go somewhere else. I said to Al, "Piedmont has a little conference room. Let's go up on the upper level and see if we can use that."

We tried that, and the Piedmont people were gracious enough to make us their guests. But when we went into the conference room to record, the people in the next room were so loud that the noise coming through the wall left us with the same distortion problems. Each show is a fairly brief radio spot, and we had set a goal of trying to finish 10 shows in 30 minutes, a two-week supply for the network. We'd never been able to complete that many back to back. But it was our ideal. The best we had ever done was 10 shows in less than an hour. There in Chicago, we spent so much time running around looking for a place to work that we were running out of time and starting to panic. We had to have 10 shows, but we had only about an hour before we had to leave. If we didn't find a good place to record these shows, we were in serious trouble because we wouldn't be able to get together again for another 10 days. We had to have these shows in the can.

Just when things looked dark, Al said, "I know exactly the place we need to go. Follow me." We went down a hallway and into a men's room in an out-of-the-way place in O'Hare airport. It wasn't much of a rest room—only one stall, a little sink and a mirror. I said, "Gee, Al, this ought to be fine, ought to work out perfect." I spread our papers and scripts out on the sink and got ready to record our first show. Things seemed perfect. We started recording and had taped about 30 to 40 seconds of the first show when a fellow came in and went into the stall. We just kept going, not missing a beat, because we figured we could still finish the show. We got no further than the 2-minute mark before the guy in the stall let one fly, with all the grunts and groans and water splashing you've ever heard from a guy in a stall.

"Don't you understand?" Al screamed at the guy. "We were in our show for two minutes."

Of course, the fellow had no idea what Al was talking about or who we were or what we were doing or why we were in there. All he knew was that he had to go to the bathroom. But Al's reaction was so violent, the poor guy barely had an opportunity to pull his pants up. He ran out the bathroom door a-flyin' with his pants still not completely zippered up. I looked at Al in complete amazement. "Al," I said, "The guy came in here to go to the bathroom. You scared the hell out of him."

Al said, "He should have known that in 20 more seconds we would have had that show done."

I said, "I'm sure that's the last thing he was thinking about."

But we couldn't let any more people interfere, Al insisted. So we ripped a sheet out of my yellow pad and wrote "Out of Order" and pasted it on the outside of the door. I thought that would give us a little time to tape. We started on our show again and had gotten about a minute recorded when a policeman came in.

"What the hell are you guys doing in here?" he asked. He didn't recognize either one of us. "Now look," he said, "I just had a complaint from a person who was in here who said you were screaming at him. I don't know what you're doing, but you get the hell out of here. You can't be in this bathroom. And who the hell put this sign up?"

He obviously meant business, so out we went. We had only 45 minutes left and had to do a show. Al thought a minute and said, "You know those offices we walked by when we came in? That's where we're going to go."

"Gee, Al," I said, "I don't know who they belong to. We better ask permission."

"We don't have time to ask permission," he said. "Let's just go in and start doing the show."

We went in. There was nobody at the secretary's desk, so I really couldn't ask for permission. Al just went into the main office and sat down. It was a beautiful office. I figured we were running out of time, so we might as well try it. All of a sudden, a well-dressed fellow came to the doorway and said, "Well, I'll be damned. It's Al McGuire and Billy Packer. What an honor to have you in my office. Fellows, whatever you need, don't worry about it. I was summoned out of a meeting and told that two guys had taken over my office. I thought you were here for a bomb threat or something."

We said, "No, no. We're just here doing our radio shows."

"Whatever you need, we'll get it for you."

He turned out to be the head of O'Hare airport. Here we were, using his office as one of our radio studios. That really worked out for us. Since that time, we've always had a nice radio studio at O'Hare anytime we need it.

Other times, our broadcasting efforts didn't have fairy-tale endings. Once we were scheduled to meet at the airport in Pittsburgh. I was on my way to a game in Syracuse, and Al was headed to North Carolina State. We worked out our schedules to take about an hour and a half in Pittsburgh, where again we hoped to knock out 10 or 12 shows. I was responsible for bringing the tape recorder and the tapes and the scripts. Except I forgot the tapes. I figured when I got to the airport I could certainly buy a tape, no problem. I got to the Pittsburgh airport, and, sure enough there was Al, punctual as ever, waiting for my flight. I told him we'd have to get a tape, and that was no problem. We were both very relaxed at that point, thinking we'd have plenty of time. But the store in the airport didn't carry tapes. Time to panic again.

I remembered there was a shopping center near the airport. Although it was rather early in the morning, we decided to get a cab and go to the shopping center, buy a tape there, and then come back to the airport to find a place to do our shows. We weren't so worried about a place to record because Al's ingenuity always seemed able to find us something. Off we went to the shopping center in a cab. First we went to K Mart, but it didn't open until 10:00. It was a little after 8:00. Our panic surged a bit. We couldn't get a tape, and we had to have these shows in the can. Then Al noticed that down the road there were some lights on at a drugstore. I thought surely we could get some tapes there. So the cabdriver took us down there.

Now, the cabdriver hadn't said anything during our drive, but he did realize who we were. He kept a low profile as Al and I talked in the back about what we were going to do. Although the lights were on in the drugstore, they weren't ready to open up. We pounded on the window, and a clerk inside waved us off and said, "No. I can't let you in. We're taking inventory in here, and I can't let you in until 10 o'clock."

We hollered back at him to get the manager. Neither of us was dressed very well that day, especially Al, who was wearing his "soft" clothes. It struck me that maybe we looked like we wanted to rob the place, two guys in vagrant clothes pounding on the window wanting in, with a cab sitting in front of the store with the engine running. But then the manager came and, much to our pleasure, recognized who we were and said, "Gee, whatever you need."

So I told him, "We need some tapes." And he said, "We've got them in packs of three." I said, "Great," and gave the guy $10. He brought the tapes to me. Al was kind of standing there. He never buys anything and has no sense whatsoever of what things cost. He watches a nickel like a hawk but never really spends anything. He probably has the deepest pockets and the shortest arms of any man who has ever walked on the face of this earth. I gave the manager $10, and when I did, he said, "Oh, that won't be necessary, sir."

But I didn't think we deserved them for nothing. I said, "No, no, we're in a real hurry. Keep the change."

Al said, "What? Are you crazy? Let's wait for the change." So the manager walked back to get the change, and I jumped in the cab and couldn't believe Al was going to worry if we got the change back from the $10. It was my money anyway. The guy came back and gave Al about 3¢ change. The tapes had cost $9.97. Al just started hollering at the guy, "What the hell? I thought you were really going to bring some change back here. I didn't know that thing cost $10. You think I would have waited out here?"

I screamed out the cab window, "Al, come on. We've got to get going here. Don't worry about the three cents; let's get moving." Finally, Al jumped into the cab, and I asked him, "OK, where are we going to record the shows?"

"Let's do them right here in the cab while we ride back to the airport," he said.

"Al," I said, "We can't possibly record the radio shows in the cab. You can hear the engine, cars beeping outside. It'll never work."

"We've never tried one like this before," he said. "Let's go ahead and try it." We did a show in the cab, one of the funniest we've ever put together. As a matter of fact, it ought to go in some radio hall of fame. I started talking about basketball, and the next thing I know Al and the cabdriver were talking about why the guy was driving such a bad cab.

The show carried on for the full two minutes, and just as we finished, the driver pulled to a screeching halt at the airport. We had one show in the can, even though it was done with traffic background noise and cab talk all the way from the drugstore to the airport.

We went into the airport and tried to do the remaining 9 shows. We went down to the flight attendants' room to do the rest, but the attendants were miffed. I couldn't believe they were really upset that we were trying to do our shows. They kept banging their lockers and coming in, making noise and laughing. They gave us no respect at all; I felt just like Rodney Dangerfield. We realized after we failed a couple of times to finish one show that it just wouldn't work. Al said, "I've got an idea. Let's get on an airplane that's not ready to take off and hasn't been loaded up with passengers. That'll be nice and quiet." We went out and got on a plane and told the flight attendant we wanted to use it to record our shows. We sat down and knocked out four or five shows until a stewardess came on and said, "Hey, we're going to have to start boarding passengers."

We sat there in the front seat, recording two more shows while the passengers boarded, with everybody walking by, seeing these two nuts in the front seat talking to one another on a recorder. The acoustics and accommodations weren't the best, but the circumstances seemed to bring out Al's street-wise best.

Then we took our radio production to New York City. Al had a game at Madison Square Garden while I did one at the Meadowlands in New Jersey. We decided to meet late at night in his hotel room over in Manhattan to do 8 or 10 shows. Al and his son, Rob, were staying at the very posh Parker Meridian, a nice room with two beds, nice furnishings, almost a suite. We finished our shows shortly after midnight. I said goodnight and went across the street to get my car out of the parking deck. But the deck was locked up for the night. I wasn't going to be able to get my car out. I wasn't worried because I knew I could get up early and drive over to the

Meadowlands and nobody would ever know I was missing. I figured I'd walk back over to the Parker Meridian and stay in Al's room. As I mentioned, his room had two beds in it, one for Robby and one for me. Al sleeps on the floor, and I knew I wouldn't be putting Robby out, so it'd work out fine. I called Al from the lobby, and he said, "Yeah, come on up. Robby's out on a date or something, but he'll be back in."

I got upstairs and found Al curled up on the floor, ready to sleep. I didn't need a key to get in because Al had the door ajar with the key hanging in it. He had left it there, because he didn't want Robby to wake him up when he came in. I put the door back the way it was with the key hanging on the outside. I knew this was New York City and you had to be careful, but that's the way Al wanted it, and probably Robby didn't have a key. I got to bed and was apparently really tired because I didn't realize that the lights were on. "Al," I asked, "can we turn off the lights?"

"No," he said, "really we're going to have to keep the lights on because I've been having a hard time sleeping through the night without having to get up and take a leak. I've been in so many different motels, I've been banging into furniture. So I leave the light on so I can see how to get to the bathroom."

I thought, "Well, OK, we can put up with that." I put my head down and figured, as tired as I was, I'd be able to sleep with the light on and the door unlatched anyway. But then I closed my eyes and realized that the shower was running. I said, "Al, who's in the shower?"

He said, "Nobody's in the shower."

I waited a moment and then asked, "Why is the water running?"

"The noise is peaceful," he said. "It helps me relax, so I just keep the shower running at night."

I thought, "Oh, boy, I'm not going to argue with him. The light's on, the door's open, and the shower's running, and I'm tired, so I'm going to bed." Sure enough, I closed my eyes and went off to sleep. I don't know how long I'd been asleep, but suddenly there was a bang on the door. I looked up, and there was a hotel policeman with his gun drawn. He said, "What the hell's going on in here?" He had found the open door with the key in the lock. He'd looked in and found one guy in the bed sleeping, one bed with nobody sleeping in it, and another guy lying on the floor in his street clothes, curled up with the bedspread from the unslept-in bed around him. And the shower was running.

I looked up and said, "Fella, let me explain it to you. The guy sleeping on the floor is Al McGuire. He doesn't sleep in beds; he only sleeps on floors. The bed that's not being used is for his son, Robby, but he hasn't come back in from a date. I'm Billy Packer, and I'm not really a guest here at the hotel. But my car's locked across the street, and I came back in to use the room. The light's on in the bathroom because my man sleeping on the floor wakes up in the middle of the night and bumps into furniture when he goes in to try to take a leak. And the shower's running because he likes peaceful noise in the background while he sleeps. Other than that, we're just regular guys."

Well, after hearing the story, the officer was so amazed that he just stopped and put his gun back in his holster and said, "Fellas, I don't care about the light. I don't care about the shower. I don't care about your weirdo friend sleeping on the floor. But please get this door locked and keep it locked because I wouldn't want anything to happen to you in here."

As he walked down the hallway, I hoped that he knew who Packer and McGuire were and that he didn't think we were total weirdos trying to do something strange in the Parker Meridian Hotel. But then again, with Al, you never know.